PRAISE FOR THE
Curious Encounters of the Human Kind
SERIES

"Most of Paul Sochaczewski's curious encounters start out as intelligent travel writing, exploring hidden corners of Asia and characters very much out of the ordinary. But this series works on a more complex level: he frequently zooms in and out of left field with a curious tangent, a sensitive reminiscence, a provocative opinion, a new way of looking at events that already are beyond most 'normal' travelers' tales. I read each story feeling refreshed, enlightened, and curious to see what the next stage of Sochaczewski's journey would bring."

—JUDITH M. HEIMANN, author of *The Most Offending Soul Alive: Tom Harrisson and His Remarkable Life* and *The Airmen and the Headhunters: A True Story of Lost Soldiers, Heroic Tribesmen and the Unlikeliest Rescue of World War II*

"What a discovery! Paul Sochaczewski is that rarest of writers who knows that the real 'Asian miracle' isn't malls or computer geeks. In his years traveling the continent, he has discovered an eternal assemblage of arcane explorers, putative emperors, frivolous mystics, sacrosanct elephants and, yes, miracle workers. When Sochaczewski finds them, in Javanese palaces or sacred forests protected by spirits, they are caviar (or sweetened bird's nest) for his fascinating portraits. A book for everyone who knows that the Mysterious East is alive and well, and more how-about-that-wonderful than you perhaps imagined."

—HARRY ROLNICK, author of *The Chinese Gourmet*, *The Complete Book of Coffee*, and *Spice Chronicles: Exotic Tales of a Hungry Traveler*

"Paul Sochaczewski skips about Asia like a Monkey God hopping from mountain to mountain, bringing back life-prolonging peaches while annoying the gatekeepers. Whatever you do, follow him on this journey!"

—LEE CHOR LIN, director of the National Museum of Singapore;
former curator of Asian Civilizations Museum – Singapore;
author of *Batik: Creating an Identity*

"Sochaczewski is a world-class searcher, reporter, and observer who has criss-crossed Asia for forty years, pausing in the most unlikely places and finding extraordinary people. The essays in this insightful and witty chronicle present a rich tapestry of eccentric nobles, self-serving naturalists, scoundrels who will make your teeth ache, celebrity monks, and memorable folks whose stories are too good to be true. But they are."

—CHRISTOPHER G. MOORE,
author of the Vincent Calvino novels and *Heart Talk*

"In this series Sochaczewski explores the hidden corners, the forgotten people, and their surprising tales. All the personal traveler's tales in these volumes are captivating, all filled with humor, drama, and insight, with an edgy take-no-prisoners voice. You won't find anything else like this on the bookshelf."

—JEFF MCNEELY, chief scientist,
International Union for Conservation of Nature

"The *Curious Encounters of the Human Kind* series is a delicious stew of improbable characters and intriguing stories, served up in thoroughly pithy style, and with a hearty dash of irreverent humour."

—TIM HANNIGAN, author of *Raffles and the British Invasion of Java*
and *Brief History of Indonesia: Sultans, Spices, and Tsunamis:
The Incredible Story of Southeast Asia's Largest Nation*

VOLUMES IN THE
Curious Encounters of the Human Kind
SERIES:

Myanmar (Burma)

Indonesia

Himalaya: India, Bhutan, Nepal

Borneo

Southeast Asia:
Thailand, Laos, Cambodia, Vietnam, the Philippines

OTHER TITLES BY PAUL SOCHACZEWSKI

Share Your Journey

An Inordinate Fondness for Beetles

The Sultan and the Mermaid Queen

Redheads

Distant Greens

Eco-Bluff Your Way to Greenism

Soul of the Tiger

CURIOUS
ENCOUNTERS
of the
HUMAN KIND

SOUTHEAST ASIA
THAILAND, LAOS, CAMBODIA, VIETNAM & THE PHILIPPINES

CURIOUS
ENCOUNTERS
of the
HUMAN KIND

SOUTHEAST ASIA

True Asian Tales of
Folly, Greed, Ambition
and Dreams

PAUL SPENCER SOCHACZEWSKI

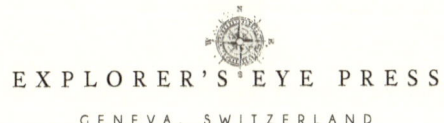

EXPLORER'S EYE PRESS

GENEVA, SWITZERLAND

Cover photo: Young lady in northeast Thailand enjoying a roasted scorpion snack.

All photos by Paul Sochaczewski, except where noted.

Jeffrey McNeely contributed to an earlier version of "Laos White Elephant Settles in After Long March."

ISBN: 978-2-940573-13-4

Published by:
Explorer's Eye Press
Geneva, Switzerland

Book design by Stacey Aaronson
Map of Southeast Asia by John Welding

Printed in the United States of America

Dedicated to the people of Asia who shared their stories,
and sometimes their homes, rice wine, termite omelets,
and dreams.

TABLE OF CONTENTS

AUTHOR'S NOTE

Some thoughts about change in Southeast Asia:

The five Southeast Asian countries highlighted in this volume include economies in different conditions of health and evolution; political systems of varying degrees of style, maturity, and reliability; and a variety of religions, belief systems, and approaches to life. In some ways there is little that connects them except propinquity. Yet in other ways they are similar, combining deep and proud cultures, diverse nature (although not always healthy or well managed), involvement in topsy-turvy geopolitical gamesmanship, and a love of a good party. Social patterns too have changed, brought on by improved infrastructure, education, healthcare, and communications. They are not always touchy-feely neighbors (witness Thailand's spat with Cambodia over ownership of an ancient Khmer temple), and Laos and Cambodia, the poor guys in the middle of the Thailand/Vietnam sandwich, are squeezed for re-sources by their larger neighbors. The Mekong River, which flows through four of the countries mentioned in this volume, is being dammed without mercy; no good news there for the downriver nations. Meanwhile, the ogre of the Middle Kingdom consumes key parts of whatever flies, swims, grows, or crawls — tigers, pangolins, elephants, and tropical hardwood feature in the shopping lists. And China is claiming economically and strategically important territories in the South China Sea, but Vietnam and the Philippines, which claim the same islands, can do little about the bullying.

In a few instances the reader may find some statistics outdated because several chapters, in simpler versions, have appeared over a period of twenty years in *The New York Times*, *International Herald Tribune*, *Wall Street Journal*, *Geographical*, *Destinasian*, *GQ*, *CNN Traveller*, *Travel and Leisure*, *Reader's Digest*, and other publications.

But while details might change, the basic truth of the human stories offered here of foibles, ambitions, and achievements remains constant.

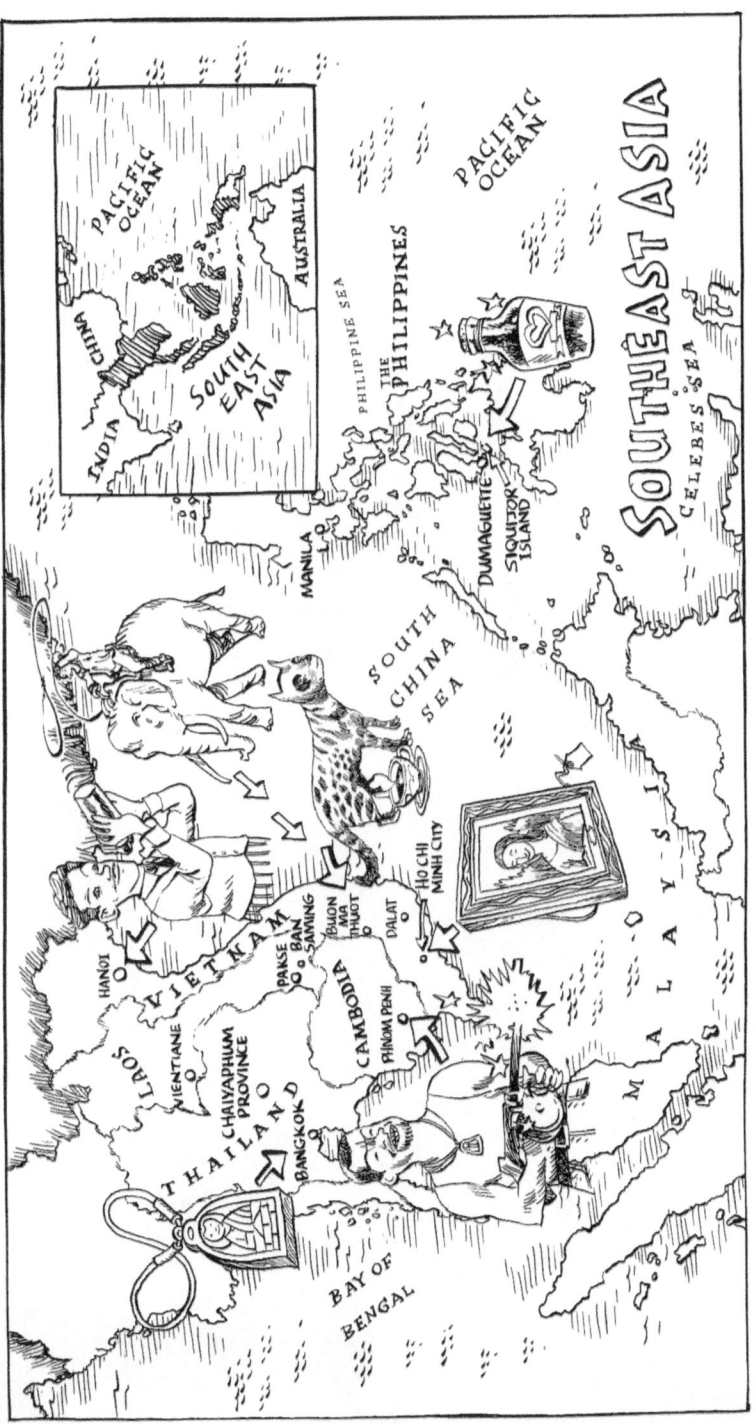

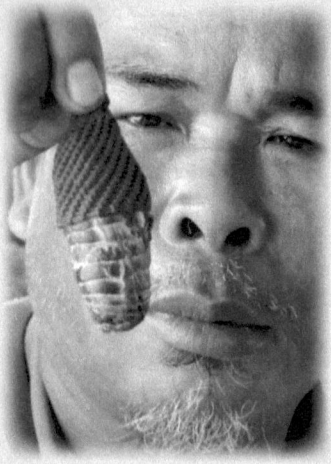

Dee Lek Khamgong, with an amulet made from fossilized
200 million-year-old freshwater shark dung.

Photo: Jeffrey A. McNeely

ᛉMULET ENVY

*Exploring Thailand's love of amulets, talismans,
and spiritual gadgets.*

CHAIYAPHUM PROVINCE, THAILAND

It's hot in Isaan, the northeastern corner of Thailand. I'm used to traveling into the forest with biologists, who appreciate an early start when the weather is a touch cooler and their subjects of investigation more likely to be active. But the group of paleontologists from Mahasarakam University I am with don't worry about a late start – first a sturdy breakfast of noodles, then a stop at a Buddhist temple to get the blessings of the abbot, then forty-five minutes bouncing up a rocky path on a wooden cart hauled by a smoke-belching tractor to get to the study site. But before we start chipping away at a shale deposit in a dried-up stream bed, we sit in the sun and enjoy a picnic of local delicacies: roast chicken, green papaya salad, and grilled grass-hoppers. The objects we're investigating aren't going to hide or wilt. We're searching for fossilized pieces of freshwater shark dung that have been around for some two hundred million years. Plenty of time for lunch.

The scientists, led by father and son Varavudh Sutee-thorn and Suravech Suteethorn, are looking for fossilized dung, or coprolites, which they hope will provide clues to better understand the wildlife that existed two hundred million years ago during the late Triassic period, when this plateau was covered in water. But my quest wasn't paleon-tology; it was what we might call amuletology – trying to understand the Thai craze for lucky charms.

Why do Thais place so much importance on talismans bearing the likeness of Lord Buddha and dozens of other Buddhist saints, Hindu gods, and animistic imaginings? All cultures have lucky charms and superstitions, but the Thais seem to lead the world in using amulets to obtain fame, fortune, and protection, not to mention lucky lottery numbers, success in exams, and lots of sex.

At the Tum Wiman Nakin temple, a peaceful small *wat* protected by a wooded cliff, the abbot, Phra Ajan Surin Thi Ta Thammo, showed us glass display cabinets filled with coprolites that villagers had given to the temple as offerings. They looked like gray stones, some as small as my pinkie nail, others as large as my thumb. A few had a distinctive spiral shape, indicating that the now-fossilized material had passed through the twisted intestines of a freshwater shark. In Thai, these coprolites are called *duk dae hin*, or "stone butterfly chrysalis," a descriptor rich in implied magic and rarity. Perhaps the form reminds believers of the Hindu conch shell, an emblem of Vishnu (when blown as a trumpet it produces the *om* vibration, which is the sound of the creation of the universe). The conch was later appropriated as one of the eight auspicious Buddhist symbols. And since the beloved king of Thailand is seen as an avatar of Vishnu, well, you do the math.

No wonder coprolites are sought after for protecting the wearer from ghosts, bullets, and snakes.

Standing to the side as we chatted with the abbot was Dee Lek Khamgong, who likes to be called Uncle Nares, a quiet, hefty, rural man-of-the-soil with small eyes who needs a bit of prodding to smile. Around his neck he wore a chain of eight large coprolites, each mounted by an amulet-artisan in a skillfully woven web of twine. Uncle Nares drove the tractor and we headed into the nearby hills.

My quest to understand Thailand's amulet culture is more than an academic exercise. I am also on the lookout for an amulet that will improve my golf game.

I went to one of my favorite amulet markets, near the Saphan Kwai Skytrain station, where each weekend several hundred dealers — both men and women — sit at kindergarten-sized tables brimming with talismans.

"What's good for golf?" I asked Khun Nok, one of my regular amulet-pushers.

She had never been asked that question and thought for a moment before handing me a popular rectangular amulet featuring Lord Buddha in a meditation posture. I recognized it as a Somdej Toh, a form created by a nineteenth-century prince who chose the austerity of the monkhood over the luxury of the royal palace. Some people credit him with starting the Thai infatuation with amulets, and original Somdej Toh amulets are by far the most valuable of the countless varieties available.

I admired the aesthetics – a meditating Buddha on a tier of three rows of plinths.

"Lord Buddha didn't play golf," I said.

"But he can provide the peace of mind you need to succeed."

IF YOU KNOW WHAT TO LOOK FOR IT ISN'T DIFFICULT to hunt coprolites. Sometimes they appear as a pimple on an exposed outcropping of rock. More often you find them by bashing away at a pile of shale with a geologist's hammer; with a bit of luck, the telltale bumps in the flat slate will be visible. The scientists found dozens in the few hours we sweated at the study site.

Uncle Nares sells the coprolites to amulet collectors; the locality is scattered with recently dug-up sites where local farmers have done their own excavations. He isn't one to give long philosophical explanations of why people pay good money for bits of fossilized dung. "Protection and good luck" he says finally, and that seems about all he is prepared to say about the matter.

Local legend claims that the coprolites can also effectively treat snake bites. Phra Ajan Surin Thi Ta Thammo, the abbot, explained that when you crush one of the coprolites and mix the powder with fresh lemon juice, the venom will become neutralized.

And that's part of the allure of all amulets in Thailand – the hope that they will produce miracles. The abbot told the story of a fellow monk (he couldn't quite remember his name), who some years ago survived a snake bite, or maybe it was a scorpion bite, he wasn't too sure, by rubbing a coprolite on the wound. Most Thais have similar stories of how their sister-in-law's hair dresser's cousin miraculously escaped a car crash that killed all the other passengers because he was wearing such-and-such an amulet.

In 2009 politician Sondhi Limthongkul survived a five-minute barrage of eighty-four bullets while he was trapped inside his SUV, escaping with only minor injuries. The street value of the three amulets he was wearing soared in value following his miraculous escape. In July 2013 the *Bangkok Post* ran a story about a police officer named Apichart Chearapanich who claimed to survive being shot four times during a drug bust because he was wearing a Khun Phantarak Ratchadej amulet at the time. In June 2014 businessman Pitak Riangsima, 40, crashed his two-million-dollar black Lamborghini on a country road. The car split in two; Riangsima walked away unscathed. He attributed the miraculous escape to his having visited a temple in Nakhon Sawan earlier that day, where a friend had given him an amulet for protection while driving long distances. No credit was given to the high-tech carbon fiber construction of the driver compartment, built to protect passengers.

Believing that some amulets can protect the people wearing them, the abbot of Wat Tum Wiman Nakin near our study site commissioned the manufacture of eighty-four thousand Buddha amulets, most of which he offered to the Thai soldiers serving in the southern part of the country, where ambushes and bombs are regular professional hazards. The recipe, which he said took five years to prepare, contains powdered coprolites, bricks from old stupas where Buddha relics are kept, dust from bones of Buddhist saints, and a mixture of holy plants and flowers. The abbot kindly gave me one of the few he had left; so far I have not been shot at or bitten by a cobra, but I am protected just in case.

Golfers, like all sportsmen, can be superstitious.

Jack Nicklaus carried three pennies in his pocket during each round, explaining, "If I carried only one penny and lost it, I'd be without a ball marker. If I had only two pennies and lost one, and a fellow player needed to borrow one to mark his ball, I'd still be out of ball markers."

Nicklaus always marked his ball with the tails side of the penny up, unlike Paul Azinger who marked his ball with the penny's head facing upward, and always with Lincoln looking toward the hole.

Chi Chi Rodriguez used three different coins to mark his ball, depending if it was an eagle, birdie, or par putt.

And what about tees?

On par threes, Jack Nicklaus would keep his good tee in his pocket and search for a broken tee on the tee box.

Doug Sanders never played a white tee, believing them to be unlucky. As he stood on the 18th-tee box of the last day of the 1970 British Open, he needed par to win the Claret Jug. The story goes that Sanders had lost his tee and a playing partner handed him a white one that Sanders decided to use, against his better judgment, to avoid slowing up proceedings. He went on to bogey the hole, famously missing a three-foot putt, and the following day lost a playoff to Jack Nicklaus (who presumably had three pennies in his pocket).

And then there's Tiger Woods's dietary regime and sartorial choices.

Tiger has a carefully worked out list of foods that he believes make him win — orange and green vegetables, fruit, turkey, baked fish, grilled chicken, skim milk, egg whites, and rice. But he swears that other foods make him lose — pizza, ice cream, cheesecake, roast beef, fried chicken, and soft drinks.

Tiger Woods follows his mother's advice to always wear a red shirt on Sunday. Like a good Asian son, Tiger's simply listening to his Thai mother, who explains, "red is a lucky color for Tiger. It brings power."

HOW DID AMULETS BECOME SO IMPORTANT IN THAILAND?

Art historian Pattaratorn Chirapravati suggests that the amulet cult began in the mid-nineteenth century during the reign of King Mongkut (Rama IV), when high-ranking

Thais acquired votive tablets that had been interred in stupas for private use in a residential "Buddha-room." The believers relied on these baked clay images of Lord Buddha, which had been pillaged from ancient holy sites, to earn merit.

Khun Nok showed me a medallion of Luang Phor Bpen, one of the superstar monks in Thailand. The cult of "guru" monks is a widespread phenomenon in Thailand and amulet aficionados know very well who the celebrity monks are; the amulets they have made and blessed command the highest prices. Some of Luang Phor Bpen's amulets show him riding a tiger, like an Asian Buddhist Roy Rogers. "Strong protection, can stop bullets," Khun Nok assured me. "Much good luck."

While it is a sin for a monk to boast of supernatural powers, apparently it is kosher for acolytes to spread the word about miracles attributed to such guru monks.

Khun Nok offered me a few other talismans bearing the likenesses of the more prominent holy men.

Next up was an amulet featuring the image of noted forest monk Luang Phor Koon, born when a deity blessed his parents for their good deeds, telling the happy couple he was giving them a gift that "will be a treasure to Buddhism."

When I demurred, Khun Nok pulled out some amulets of Luang Phor Hong, who encouraged the production of amulets bearing his likeness, and who even offered a guarantee that his amulets would made the wearer bullet-proof — "If my amulets do not work, may I die one hundred times a day." Khun Nok said Luang Phor Hong's blessings were so powerful that

Prince Norodom Sihanouk of neighboring Cambodia had attributed the blessings of the great monk to his success in regaining control of his country.

"Here's Luang Poo Jiam — surely you know him," Khun Nok asked. "Well, not really ..." She explained that amulets bearing his likeness and blessing had just saved the lives of some soldiers in the south. She wasn't too sure about the details, but I found the story in a recent edition of the *Bangkok Post*, in which an army private named Kiattisak Tangthong said the amulet "will protect me from harm and also from punishment." He added, somewhat obtusely, "Failing to wear it will put me in jail for three nights." It seems that Major General Thawatchai Samutsakorn, who issued the must-wear order, said that a bus carrying soldiers was attacked by terrorists. Fifteen soldiers who carried the amulets in their rucksacks were injured. The others who wore the amulets as necklaces were unharmed. The amulet has become standard equipment.

The names of these monks might not mean anything to non-Thais, but they are among the Hall of Fame monks whose amulets are worth the most. How wonderfully Hollywood that the most powerful (and therefore most expensive) amulets have been blessed by, and feature the images of superstar monks, legendary wise men with reputations as big as the secular Western world's Muhammad Ali, Elvis, Einstein and Pelé.

SEEKING GOOD LUCK THROUGH A TALISMAN IS A FIRST cousin to a miracle.

Take the case of Arthit Chairob. He is a part-time guide at Bangkok's Golden Teak Museum. On the morning of May 8, 2010, while waiting for the first Saturday visitors, he examined the holiest object in the museum – a twenty-centimeter tall gold chedi (stupa) that contains relics of Lord Buddha. Arthit told me he spotted what he thought was a "dead insect" semi-hidden in the separation between the small chedi and the larger shrine. He called for the cleaner, but religious experts came instead, had a look, and declared that the small pile of maroon crystals (similar in color to a monk's robe and about the size of grains of sea salt) were miraculous evidence of a holy artifact reproducing itself. Buddha's relics had self-cloned.

No scientific tests were requested to clarify the composition of the red crystals. But that hardly matters; a scientific analysis is against the spiritual nature of religion, in which miracles are black and white – a believer has faith in his heart while a skeptic insists on a left-brain Cartesian scientific explanation. In Thai Buddhism, as in virtually every major religion in most every country, such difficult-to-explain phenomena are the take-it-on-faith pizazz that keeps the faithful coming back.

Such happenings occupy the twilight realm of spirit and imagination when a curious situation, super-heated in the athanor of ritual and desire, undergoes an alchemy and morphs into a phenomenon, which in turn evolves into a miracle that provides the underpinning of a complex creature called religion.

I knew Khun Nok was picking and choosing, trying to be helpful. She was ignoring dozens of other forms of amulets and talisman — where was the phallus-shaped phalad khik, *the metal-rod* takrut, *the oversized* Jatukam Ramathep *(in September 2007, at the height of what is called the "Jatukam craze," one wat advertised its get-rich-quick medallions on the side of the country's tallest skyscraper, the Baiyoke Tower), the circular dharma wheel, the gaudy butterfly-patterned Kruba Krissana (a genuine Kruba Krissana is said to never lose its sweet scent), the goofy-faced Opakut? She could just as easily have shown me the* Phra Kring, *which rings like a bell; historian Srisakara Vallibhotama suggests that this amulet, distributed by monks from Cambodia in the nineteenth century, helped create the current cult of commercial amulets. Thailand's natural world might be losing biodiversity at a frenzied pace, but there is no shortage of amulet diversity.*

THE CATHOLIC CHURCH, FOR INSTANCE, BASES ITS legitimacy on miracles — a virgin birth, walking on water, turning water into wine. And the criteria for becoming a Catholic saint is that the individual has to have performed at least two miracles *after* his or her death.

How can a miracle, which by definition is beyond logical definition, be scientifically explained? Two different jurisdictions are involved — the emotional and the rational. It's a bit like love: a person doesn't go through a left-brain checklist ("doesn't smoke, spells correctly, likes

Mexican food") in order to "prove" her emotions. Consider the case of Mother Teresa, the tireless symbol of Catholic charity and selflessness. Most people applaud her humanity and selfless spirit. But when Mother Teresa's miracles are questioned things get messy. She earned her beatification, the third of four steps en route to Roman Catholic sainthood, because it is claimed a beam of light emanating from a locket containing her picture cured an Indian woman, Monica Besra, of cancer. However, Ranjan Mustafi, Besra's doctor, told *The New York Times* that the woman's cyst was caused by tuberculosis and was not malignant. "It was not a miracle," he said. "She took medicines for nine months to one year." Besra's husband added: "My wife was cured by the doctors and not by any miracle."

It's a very simple equation. One believes in the inexplicable, or one doesn't.

Khun Nok glanced at a rak yom *amulet — representations of twin infant boys entwined and sealed in a capsule containing holy oil. And I was happy she didn't offer it to me. Virtually all the amulets I've handled have, for me, no innate power; I view them simply as curiosities. Perhaps that is an inability on my part to sense the inner energy that "good" amulets generate. But once I did bargain for a* rak yom *amulet and it just didn't feel right having it in my home. I was aware of tales of how the best* rak yom *amulets are made from embryos and bones of dead monks, and their preparation involves graveyard incantations; ownership of these amulets requires regular, strict obeisance. The* rak yom *amulet made me nervous, and I put it into a shrine erected in a large tree at an intersection in my neighborhood, there to emit whatever power it had with other likeminded amulets placed in the branches.*

MAYBE THERE ARE TIBETAN MONKS WHO CAN TELEPORT. Maybe there are Indian sadhus who can survive frigid weather by self-heating their bodies. Maybe there are healers who can tap into energy fields and with a glance cure people of "incurable" diseases. Maybe there are men and women who can channel ancestors and aliens, who can see the future and look into people's souls. Maybe there are folks who have deep wisdom and gifts that are beyond the ken of most mortals. And maybe a talisman bearing the image of these folks can help ordinary people enjoy Cosmic Insurance. Maybe. Who knows? What if?

Some righteous Thai Buddhist friends accuse me of not taking this amulet business seriously. A fair comment because I really don't know what to make of all this. I think I am rational and guided by science. But of course there are incidents in our lives that are impossible to explain.

So, believe in a superstition and it just might work. Don't believe it and, who knows, it still might work.

Steve Cohen, a psychotherapist and president of the California-based Shivas Irons Society, which promotes the "transformational" elements of golf, suggests that superstition and ritual are part of "the basis of all religion, and embedded in every culture. Superstition can help you get rid of those things that create anxiety, like a shank in golf." In other words, we need superstitions and religion because there is so much in the world that we can't explain except by invoking divine causes.

As a weekend duffer I can fully understand the desire to seek the support of a benevolent outside agency. Why does one long putt go in while another circumnavigates the hole without falling? Why do some horrible slices land on a nice patch of grass with a clear opening to the green, and some wind up behind a cactus? Is this due to luck? And if so, can we improve our luck?

Fred Shoemaker, a professional golfer who is founder and director of Extraordinary Golf, an academy and teaching center that he says creates "an environment in which a golfer's instincts and awareness lead to the true source of power and proficiency," doesn't condone cultivating superstitions but sees that they can be beneficial for some golfers. "Superstitions, and the resulting rituals, are a way for golfers to address their 'self-doubt' and allow the golfer to be present, instead of worrying about what might happen in the future," Shoemaker says. He adds that golfers might just be more superstitious than other athletes because "golf is a slow, non-reactive sport [unlike, say, tennis], with more opportunities for the golfer's mind to interfere with the action."

SOME PSYCHOLOGISTS SUGGEST THAT SUPERSTITIONS OF any kind can raise stress and anxiety levels. Take the number four. "Four" is a bad number for Chinese, because the Mandarin word for four, *sì*, is a homonym for the word for death, with similar pronunciations and connotations in Cantonese, Japanese, and Korean. For Chinese- and Japanese-Americans, the fear of the number four – clinically described as tetraphobia – can be a real killer. Consider: on the fourth of each month cardiac deaths for Chinese- and Japanese-Americans spike seven percent compared to other days, according to a 2002 study by a team of scientists at the University of California–La Jolla.

Throughout Asia there can be a perverse belief that bad luck for some can bring good luck to others.

In Malaysia it's not unusual for people to buy lottery tickets bearing the license plate number of a car that had been totaled in a devastating crash – no blacking out of the gory newspaper photographs in Malaysia.

And shortly after Malaysian Airlines flight 17 was shot down in eastern Ukraine in July 2014, Malaysian gambling operators reported they had sold out of lottery numbers 1717 and 777. Why these numbers?

The flight number was 17, it was a Boeing 777 manu-factured in July (month seven) 1997, and it had seventeen years of service before it crashed on July 17 en route to Kuala Lumpur from Amsterdam.

Such beliefs imply that good luck charms can work

passively, without the hassle of tiresome prayers or rituals or payments. Niels Bohr, the Danish Nobel Prize-winning physicist, kept a horseshoe over his lab door, noted David Phillips, the lead author of the La Jolla study about the fatal effects of the number four on Asian Americans. According to Philips, "Somebody said [to Bohr], 'Surely you don't believe this superstition brings you good luck?' He said, 'I don't believe in it, but I'm told it works even if you don't believe in it.'"

Virtually everyone, virtually everywhere, believes in superstition and good/bad luck. In the West this might take the form of not crossing the path of a black cat, or not walking under a ladder, or not stepping on a crack in the sidewalk. We knock on wood. Many Catholics wear a cross and have a Saint Christopher's medal in their cars to ensure safe journeys – I'm reminded of the song from *Cool Hand Luke*: "I don't care if it rains or freezes/Long as I have my plastic Jesus/Riding on the dashboard of my car." Jews might wear a Star of David or place a mezuzah near their front door; Muslims might wear talismans containing Qur'anic inscriptions. It's a way of saying I belong to a particular religious/ethnic tribe and I buy into the rituals and ceremonies that might, maybe, who knows, give me a break in life.

For the big "un-understandable" many people turn to formal religion. There is a fuzzy continuum between the power-infused sacred paraphernalia of formal religions and many secular good luck charms. Is there really so much difference between Tiger Woods wearing a *sai-sin* Buddhist cord bracelet offered by a monk and Rickie Fowler marking his Pro V1x with "4.13," a reference to his favorite passage from Philippians: "I can do everything through him who gives me strength." All part of the same rainbow continuum. Folks might believe in a Hairy Thunderer or a Cosmic Muffin, an Earth Mother or a Good Luck Goblin. They're all ways to seek higher intervention in order to avoid problems and bring luck.

Do superstitions really work? Well, like so many things concerning the human psyche, if you think it will help, it probably does.

Too many options. All made sense yet none of them felt right.

"What about an amulet with Phra Reussi," I suggested, referring to the bearded, goofy-hatted hermit monk who helps people find wisdom.

"Yes, he could help," Khun Nok said. "But so could Phit Tha," she said, referring to the image of a monk covering his eyes, as in "the monkey who sees no evil."

"Isn't it good to see where the ball goes?" I asked.

"Don't be so literal," she scolded. "He covers his eyes so that he is not distracted. Good for focusing. Good for luck."

"Well, not getting distracted is good," I conceded.

"Then maybe an amulet of Phra Sankachai would be helpful." Khun Nok explained that Sankachai was a ridiculously handsome disciple of Lord Buddha and was so distracted by the gazes of lust-in-their-hearts female acolytes

that he turned himself into an unattractive fat monk so he could meditate in peace.

I patted my hard-to-control stomach, shaped in that no-man's land somewhere between a six-pack and a keg. No, I don't think a fat and unattractive (albeit devoted) monk should be my personal golf role model.

I'M SKEPTICAL ABOUT FORMAL RELIGIONS BUT SEE THEIR purpose; it's the only point on which I agree with Karl Marx. But to each his own, as long as the believer does no evil and doesn't impose his doctrine on others.

And I believe that most of the followers and clerics of the main religions *are* basically decent people. It's when a cleric goes rogue that the newspaper headlines heat up – choose any religion and choose any part of the world and you'll see aberrant religious leaders of all stripes and belief systems abusing children, getting involved with dirty politics, cheating people, violating their avowed principles, preaching violence and hatred.

My dilemma is that I have a superficial knowledge of amulets but am out of my depth when the discussion turns esoteric, as it usually does. My taxi-driver-compatible Thai is similarly basic, and my pronunciation is just good enough to indicate my interest; after that I have to smile like a dummy and make appropriate noises when the person I'm speaking with starts telling me about miracles he's heard of and temples he's visited.

IN A 2010 STUDY KASIKORN RESEARCH CENTER estimated that the Thailand amulet market, including manufacturing, transport, advertising, publishing, and rental of retail space, was worth more than one billion dollars annually, helped by the industry exemption from tax, and growing at ten to twenty percent annually.

That doesn't count the money given to Buddhist temples. One estimate is that each year the Thai public donates around $40 billion to the country's 37,075 *wats*. According to research by Nada Chansom of Thailand's National Institute of Development Administration, most temples have rudimentary or no accounting systems, and there is no monitoring or auditing of temple finances. For some temples, amulet sales contribute huge amounts – Miti Ruangkritya, a Thai journalist who reports on what he calls "Buddhist Commercialism," estimates that amulets blessed by Luang Phor Khoon, one of Thailand's most sacred (and famed) saints, earn as much as $30 million a year for his home temple – Wat Ban Rai in Nakhon Rachasima province.

With the combination of Thai generosity and human folly, it's not surprising that scoundrels like Nen Kham rise to lick the cream.

As every Thai knows, a monk takes a lifelong vow to be celibate (he is not even allowed to touch a woman accidentally or to take an offering from a woman's hands). He vows to live a simple and respectful life, to avoid tobacco, alcohol, and gambling. Most monks follow these rules, more or less, but more than a few push the envelope on what they perceive as acceptable behavior.

Nen Kham stretched the boundaries to a headline-grabbing extent.

Nen Kham, whose formal name was Phra Wirapol Sukphol, was a monk from Si Sa Ket province in the northeast. In mid-2013 it was reported that he had sex with at least eight women while he was a monk. That he bought a private jet and a mansion in the United States. That he slept with a minor and fathered her child. That he was involved in drugs and money laundering. He was defrocked in July 2013.

And where did Nen Kham get his seed money? From devotees who feel they earn merit by giving alms to monks.

Now, most alms-giving is modest and well inten-tioned – in front of my house in Bangkok, near the center of the city, each morning at dawn a few saffron-clad monks walk down the street with their begging bowls. Some folks offer the monks neat plastic bags filled with rice and curry. When asked, the monks sit and give the seeker-of-boons a blessing, or answer her questions: why does her husband cheat on her, how should she discipline a wayward daughter, and any hot tips for the lottery this month? All very communal and done in good spirit. The monks are fulfilling their responsibility to their community while the people who give them donations are earning merit.

Some folks seek merit with bigger donations. In 2014

a generous merit-seeker gave a Buddhist nun a new white Porsche Cayman. A photo of the nun driving the car hit the Thai blogosphere, forcing the National Office of Buddhism to issue a warning to the nun, from Wat Tham Khwan Muang in Chumphon Province, to adopt a more frugal lifestyle, while asking the public to only make "appropriate donations to religious leaders."

European collectors (well, me and my friends) are more interested in aesthetic considerations than in potential miracles. One foreign friend only collects images of the Buddha with animals. Another friend likes attractive images of Mae Thoranee, an Earth goddess who saved Lord Buddha from drowning while he was meditating (it's a complicated story). A third seeks sleek, stylized images of Buddha that remind her of Modigliani drawings. We are interested in amulets for all the wrong reasons — we value them as art or collect them as anthropological curiosities; this might explain why most Thais don't waste their time to elaborate on the subtleties of amulets to foreigners.

By contrast, the deep-pocket Thai collector values an amulet based on provenance — which monk is featured on the amulet, which wat manufactured it, how many were made, and what anecdotes have been told about its efficacy.

THE FOLKS OF THAILAND SEEM TO HAVE PERFECTED THE trifecta of combining superstition, religion and commercialism.

I get a feeling for the scale of the amulet business when I attend amulet fairs and competitions, held about twice a month in locations throughout the country. These events are a source of pride for cities as large as Bangkok and Chiang Mai as well as for small towns that are far off the radar. They attract hundreds of dealers and thousands of buyers. More important is the competition itself, where hopeful amulet owners submit their treasures to be examined by dozens of experts, who are ensconced in a protected space that can be as large as several tennis courts. The best amulets and statues win certificates and ribbons; to push a simile, the Thai amulet collector entering a competition is like an American youngster from Iowa, perhaps a member of a 4-H Club, bringing his favorite heifer to the state fair in hopes of earning a medal. But winning an amulet competition is about more than bragging rights; a prize-winning amulet can bring a substantial increase in its resale value.

And how much are valuable amulets worth? When the new martial-law government was put in place in 2014, each government minister was asked to list his or her assets. The new tourism and sports minister, Kobkarn Wattana-vrangkul, noted that she owned eighteen amulets worth about $1.9 million, roughly $110,000 each. She also noted that she owned four Buddha statues worth a cool million, and nine handbags worth $75,000. How, I wonder, can a handbag be worth more than $8,000?

It's tough to do research; English-language reports of Thailand's infatuation with amulets tends toward the gee-whiz end of the spectrum, partly because Thai experts (and everyone seems to be an expert) are reluctant to share information with foreigners, who the Thais are convinced will never understand "Thainess."

A few English-language sites exist, catering to amulet buyers in Malaysia, Singapore, and Hong Kong, but the vast majority of magazines and websites devoted to Thai amulets are in Thai.

In an ideal world I could simply click the "translate" button and read about these treasures. But like many things in Thailand, the deck is stacked against people who can't read Thai. I don't know if the problem lies with the trans-lation software, the arcane vocabulary of the original texts, or a nefarious plot to deprive foreigners of knowledge that defines Thainess. Here are some descriptions of amulets for sale, which sound like inscrutable zen koans, courtesy of the combined skills of www.prapantip.com and Google:

> The clay tablets of the father superscript tax than Stinky Monkey timber port in the census [only $200]

> Leo Kwan morale pincers original father of three floating body standing leg mauled prey, never worn a poppy on old age.

> The pump albino grandfather two asterisks after copper bell bottoms silver fillings.

The meat was a little angel.

The "descent Millionaire" dark meat buried talents of a dungeon.

I closed my eyes I love the mix of glass powder type mold fungi.

Grandmother's crestfallen face after the 2508 Act still leaves the Serbian equation. [$650]

MERIT IS A DIFFICULT TERM FOR ME TO UNDERSTAND. Is merit the same as charity? If I donate money to, say, a foundation that gives education to street kids (as I do), what is my motive? Do I do so anonymously? Or do I put my name on the donation so folks will know that I made an effort? Do I expect anything in return – a thank you note, a tax write-off, a blessing?

Or do I expect "merit"?

Earning merit is an elusive concept that I translate as earning karma points. And I'm not just talking about Thai Buddhists – this is a cross-cultural, cross-ethnic consideration. By doing good works (which could be as simple as giving an orange-colored plastic bucket filled with detergent, toothpaste, and fruit-drink syrup to a Buddhist monastery in Thailand), isn't there an expectation that somewhere, some Cosmic Accountant will make a note in the Cosmic Ledger, just as that Christmas song that warns "Santa is making a list and checking it twice ..."? Collect enough karma points and you will be rewarded in your next life. In Thailand it is thought that only men can graduate to nirvana, so for women a healthy accumulation of karma points might help them come back in the next life as a guy. For a Thai man, those karma points might be enough for him to graduate into a heavenly afterlife.

It's similar to the way my suburban mother used to collect Green Stamps from our local supermarket; fill up one book and you get a free toaster, two books and you get a lawn mower.

The trouble is that there's no website telling you how many karma points you earn for each spiritual transaction, nor how many you might need to achieve your desired goal. Very confusing. The only way to be somewhat sure (and you will never be absolutely sure until you die, at which point you won't remember what all the fuss was about to begin with) is to be generous with the folks who have a hotline to the Buddha – in this case, monks.

I was becoming bewildered, if not bewitched. I had my two-dollar jeweler's loupe out and was examining the talismans with great intent but little profound knowledge. I carry the loupe, fingering it like prayer beads, to pretend I know what I'm doing and to garner a touch of undeserved respect from passersby. Not much different from my on-the-golf-course behavior, actually.

We were jostled by folks visiting a neighboring stand who were rummaging through boxes filled with amulets that cost less than a dollar each. "Fakes," Khun Nok muttered, but that didn't stop the mostly male collectors from hopefully examining each piece, the Thai equivalent of American memorabilia collectors sorting through a box of old baseball cards in search of a Jackie Robinson rookie card. I remembered when I was a kid and collected ancient Roman coins: some dealers would offer job lots — say fifty coins for ten dollars — with the enticing come-on: "Gold has been found in lots like this."

"Be careful when you rent amulets," my Thai friends warn. My friends are referring to the widespread counterfeiting of valuable amulets, which can go for many thousands of dollars. But they are also referring to the concept that one never "buys" an amulet but instead "rents" it. An individual can't own something that is sacred. It's best to be given an amulet; next best is to "rent" it, using the verb chao.

My friends pull out some of the dozens of amulet magazines that tell collectors what to look for. At random I open a page that offers dozens of tips on how to tell a genuine Somdej Toh, with advice like: "The left armpit is slightly higher than the right one" and "The first base [plinth] on which Lord Buddha sits resembles a Chinese junk boat."

And chemistry is involved. It is said a genuine Somdej Toh is made from a cocktail of ingredients including powdered seashells, gold dust, burned blessed scrolls, flowers from altars of holy temples, and leftover rice from his begging bowl. Macbeth, anyone?

Thailand's legal system can be as flexible as bamboo, but the crime of amulet forgery is sometimes taken seriously.

In 2014 former Pheu Thai Party MP Chaowarin Latthasaksiri was sentenced to a year in prison in 2007 for producing and selling forty thousand *Jatukarm Ramathep* amulets, falsely claiming the talismen had been blessed at the Temple of the Emerald Buddha. According to the *Bangkok Post*, then-senator Chaowarin made headlines in 2001 when he claimed to have uncovered billions of dollars worth of World War II booty left behind by the Japanese army in a cave near the Thai-Burma border. The claim fooled the then-prime minister Thaksin Shinawatra into flying to the supposed treasure site by helicopter, only to emerge red-faced and empty-handed.

A nasty man did something nasty to a Thai friend. My friend contemplated confrontation. He contemplated hiring a bunch of thugs. He contemplated a lawsuit. He contemplated sending his nemesis a dead rat in the mail. He contemplated visiting a sorcerer who said he could put a spell on the blaggard. In the end he followed the advice of his Thai friends who said, "leave him alone. If he's a bad man, he'll be punished in the next life."

I confess, I'm not totally convinced by this "bad deeds will come back to punish you" approach to life.

But plenty of Thais are. They'll try to make merit by helping others. They'll also try to make merit by contributing money and goods to temples. The logic is that helping a monk is a good thing, therefore the more you do the more you get back.

But it's not an instant payback. If you buy a lottery ticket, you know pretty quickly whether you are a millionaire or a sucker.

No, with merit you have to be patient. That's what the circle of life/death/rebirth is all about. Trusting that the deeds we do today come back in the next life to either bless our lives or bite us in the ass.

Isn't that what all religions are offering? *Believe in what we say, and even though we can't prove it, you will be rewarded in the next life. We're religious people and wear distinctive costumes and chant in ancient languages and have a hotline to the cosmos. Trust us.*

And the scoundrel who had wronged my friend? He died a couple years later of a painful throat cancer.

So many paradoxes, so many explanations, so little certainty.

I tell my friends that I'm only interested in attractive amulets that cost a few dollars. They shake their heads to show their dismay that I'm not "serious." A cheap amulet is a toy; an expensive amulet has power. Everybody knows that.

VIRTUALLY EVERY *WAT* IN THE COUNTRY MANUFACTURES and sells amulets. They make amulets so that folks will keep an image of Buddha close and can remember Buddha's precepts. They make amulets to earn money to pay for the *wat*'s operating expenses.

Here's the paradox. As I understand it, a good Buddhist is expected to be humble, benevolent, and place more importance on living a good moral life than living a life measured in material gains.

But these noble precepts seem to be sublimated by the desire for "good luck." And what is this elusive concept? It could be protection against bad things that are the bane of everyday life — illness, accidents, enemies. And it could be helping the wearer "win," which means winning the lottery, or getting a good job, or passing an exam. In other words, accumulating wealth and success. And amulets are worn by the good guys *and* the bad guys, with the distinction between the two often gray and muddled. The streets of Bangkok are littered with gangsters, pimps, corrupt cops, and dirty politicians who serenely wear their Buddha amulets. The amulet is an equal-opportunity enhancer of whatever one's goal might be.

THE AMULET-BOON BUSINESS GEARS UP AT THE temples themselves. The stakes rise in direct proportion to the size and gaudiness of the Buddha images. And with a more elaborate sacred space comes more elaborate ways to commercialize the encounter.

At the Saman Rattanaram temple east of Bangkok, thousands of visitors pray to a twenty-four-meter long reclining pink Ganesha statue, said to be the biggest of its kind in the world, for good luck. A *Bangkok Post* article noted that the temple managers have decided that folks should whisper their requests to the rat, Ganesha's vehicle, and next to a large statue of the holy rodent they have placed a money box labeled, in Thai: "Give bribe to the all-seeing rat, every wish will be granted." Critics are offended by the use of the word *sinbon* (bribe – the same word one might use to convince a policeman not to give you a ticket) and not the more common term *thamboon* (donate, or make merit). "Our society has the nature of glorifying sacred objects to create a trend for the sake of religion-related businesses," says Komkrit Uitekkeng of Silpakorn University. "I understand the amulet industry needs something new that has marketability, so they are trying to elevate Ganesh up to a special position." Komkrit added that "The problem with some Thai Buddhists is how they are always looking for someone special to be their hero, to help them solve their problems, even though Buddhism teaches them to rely on themselves." The make-a-wish visitors interviewed in the newspaper article about the "bribery" phenomenon couldn't care less about semantics. They paid their money, whispered their desires to the rat, and expected a return on investment.

<hr />

Finally, a dozen other amulets later, Khun Nok arrived at the amulet I knew she would have to arrive at. Ganesha, the elephant-headed son of Shiva and Parvati. Ganesha, the most beloved and commonly invoked god in the Hindu pantheon. Ganesha, the cuddliest of the gods and one of the most popular in equal-opportunity Thailand, which, although predominantly Buddhist, maintains a deep respect for the Hindu deities.

Ganesha is known as the "remover of obstacles."

I already own several dozen Ganesha amulets and statues, collected from Thailand, India, Sri Lanka, Nepal, and Indonesia. But a guy can't have too many Ganeshi, so I rented from Khun Nok a cute little amulet of Ganesha balanced on one leg and dancing a little jig. Sort of like he just chipped in from off the green to win the U.S. Open.

PHALLUS-FEARING DEMONS BE GONE

Sometimes the definition of a talisman's success is the absence of trouble. That's what happened with my Bhutanese *po*.

During a trek in central Bhutan, I became intrigued by the phallus images, called *po* in Dzonghka, Bhutan's national language, which protect many Bhutanese houses. Dasho Karma Ura, head of the Center for Bhutan Studies, describes these decorations as "exuberant and gifted penises, always slightly askew and sometimes frothy."

They trace their origin to a fifteenth- to sixteenth-century Buddhist yogi named Lama Drukpa Kunley. He was to phallus popularity what Brigitte Bardot was to the bikini. Unlike the gentle and placid approach of mainstream Buddhist missionaries, Lama Drukpa Kunley proselytized through anarchy, shock, and awe. He believed that only by spotlighting the absurdity of all fixed, man-made rules, and by forcing the student to abandon all ideas of predictability and emotional security, can people become wise enough to understand the "crazy wisdom" of Buddhist enlightenment.

Lama Drukpa Kunley, enfant terrible of Buddhist missionaries, seducer of women (including his own mother, but it was for her own good, he argued), famously subdued the female demons of Bhutan with his "flaming thunderbolt." He exemplified the tantric belief that carnal relations can be the gateway to enlightenment, and was not hesitant to enlighten as many women as possible.

So I commissioned a twice life-size wooden pink phallus with a knife-like crosspiece symbolizing "cutting through ignorance" (or maybe it represents circumcision, who knows?). At a glance the talisman looked like a stubby, not-quite-completed B-52. It had a yellow ribbon at the business end to represent enlightened anti-demon ejaculate. "Will this protect my house in Bangkok?" I asked Karma, the carpenter who made the flaming thunderbolt. "Should do," he said, but I could see he had no experience with transboundary flying phalluses. Just to be sure, we had it blessed by a lay monk.

On our return to Thailand in May 2010, the people of Bangkok were tensing for a battle between rival Red Shirts and Yellow Shirts. We carefully unpacked our Flying Phallus and hung it in our Thai garden. A military intervention seemed certain, and just a kilometer away armed soldiers were gathering for a final showdown with the implacable demonstrators.

While central Bangkok burned, life on our little *soi* continued relatively undisturbed. The noodle guy in front of our house stayed open, as did the grilled-chicken lady, the vegetable seller, and the motorcycle-taxi drivers. The cat slept peacefully. I'm not too sure that the sword helped us to cut through ignorance to achieve wisdom, but I'm pretty certain that at least the phallus-fearing demons went elsewhere.

Ama Kong blowing a buffalo horn, alerting hunters
to the presence of wild elephants.

LAST GREAT ELEPHANT HUNTER ACHIEVES ENDOCHINE GLORY

He's notched up 298 pachyderms,
and a lucrative product endorsement contract.

BUON MA THUOT, VIETNAM

tardom can be defined in many ways. For Ama Kong it is a number, 298, the sum of wild elephants he has captured.

Now ninety, with failing eyesight but still with a healthy head of hair, Ama Kong is the Michael Jordan of elephant hunters. He is, by his accounts, the second most successful elephant hunter in the country (his late uncle, Ama Krong, holds the title, with four hundred eighty-seven animals). Ama Kong has hobnobbed with royalty and government dignitaries. He proudly shows a nasty groin scar from a tusking – a badge of honor. And Ama Kong has his own signature brand of medicinal wine, the Vietnamese equivalent of having a sneaker named after you.

The gold lettering on the wine's striking red box reads: "Good for strengthening a man's back and kidneys," an Asian euphemism indicating that this is a powerful sex tonic.

And Ama Kong is walking proof that his wine works, having sired twenty-one children with four wives. The tonic might also explain his fine memory, since he is able to remember the names and birthdays of his spouses and offspring, including the youngest, a curious girl of seven named H'Bup Eban, who can't resist clambering onto dad's lap. But there are some things that even herbal tonics can't fix – his upper teeth are bright, intact, and obviously false compared to the red rotting stumps of his lower teeth, destroyed by years of chewing betel.

Ama Kong is likely to be the last elephant hunter superstar – since the animals are protected by Vietnamese law, fewer young people learn the skills today, not to mention there are far fewer elephants around to catch.

Vietnam's elephant population has declined drama-tically in recent years, falling from a maximum estimated population of two thousand wild animals in 1980 to just one hundred fourteen in 2000.

The domesticated elephant population has similarly declined. In Dak Lak province, where Ama Kong lives, located in the Vietnamese Central Highlands near the Cambodian border, there were some three hundred domesticated elephants in 1990; that number decreased to just one hundred thirty-eight in 2000.

But how exactly do you capture a wild elephant?

Moving slowly (when you're ninety, arthritis seeps in, even with the help of medicinal wine), Ama Kong demonstrates the procedure.

First he blows on a trumpet made of buffalo horn to

seek the support of the forest spirits. He then explains how he would go into the forest with several domesticated elephants (always an odd number of animals – odd numbers indicate male power; even numbers female) and look for a herd of wild pachyderms. The domestic elephants are Judas elephants, he explains, since they are able to mingle with the wild herd, even when *mahouts* sit atop their necks. The group tries to isolate a baby or juvenile ("easier to train than an adult" and a whole lot easier to catch). Using a kind of cowboy lasso technique, Ama Kong shows how he would catch the prey's foot with a rattan loop attached to a long stick. The lasso was attached to a hundred meter-long handmade rope crafted from water buffalo skin, and as the baby elephant ran it would get hopelessly entangled in the trees. The domesticated elephants would then take over and escort the kidnapped baby as far as possible from the wild herd. When the elephant hunters camped at night, they lit fires and beat gongs to frighten away the wild elephants that had come to rescue the crying infant.

Ama Kong has also captured eight rare white elephants, which he describes as being "like the French because they have yellow eyes and fair skin." Because of the scarcity of white elephants and their importance in Buddhist cosmology, which in turn consolidates the power of kings, these animals brought him into contact with royalty from Thailand, Laos, and Cambodia.

In 1996, at the age of eighty-one, Ama Kong captured his last elephant. This was five years after his hunting ground was turned into a national park and elephants were declared a protected species.

"It's a shame the government won't let us hunt anymore," he says. "I'm still strong enough to lead a group of hunters into the forest."

VIETNAM'S ELEPHANTS AT WAR

What do you do with a wild elephant once you catch it?

Domestic elephants have been used for centuries in Southeast Asia as tanks, tractors, and executioners.

They have also played a major role in military battles; Alexander the Great, when confronted by a team of combat elephants in northern India in 326 B.C.E, remarked, "At last I have met with a danger suitable to the greatness of my soul."

More recently, domestic elephants played a role in the Vietnam War (called the American War by Vietnamese). And the Central Highlands, where Ama Kong's village lies, was a Viet Cong stronghold.

Elephants were used in battle by the Viet Minh during the French Indochina War and later by both Viet Cong and South Vietnamese forces during the Vietnam War. An American helicopter gunship pilot told me that he had orders to not only bomb pack elephants being used to supply Viet Cong troops along the Ho Chi Minh Trail, but to kill any wild elephants he saw since they had the potential to be caught and turned into enemy assets. He said he had nightmares for months due to the screams he heard of dying elephants.

Although the U.S. Army noted the usefulness of the elephant as a pack animal, the Army warned – in a field manual distributed to Special Operations Forces – that the giant herbivores "should not be used by U.S. military personnel" due to their endangered status and the inherent dangers in riding them.

The use of napalm, Agent Orange, and other defoliants during the war resulted in loss of wild elephant habitat in the country, one reason that Vietnam's wild elephant population has dropped to less than a hundred animals today.

Boun Somsy, with a painting of his white elephant that was
liberated by the wife of the country's first president.

LAOS WHITE ELEPHANT SETTLES IN AFTER LONG MARCH

*Communist leaders use the animal to co-opt
the power and prestige of Buddhist kings.*

BAN SAMING, LAOS

apturing a rare white elephant usually brings luck and fame, and it did for Boun Somsy, at least for a while.

Then, as sometimes happens, a couple of wannabe royals stepped in and rained on his parade.

This is a tale of prophetic (and sensual) dreams, an unexpected windfall, how an areligious communist government usurped a potent religious symbol, and, as is so often the case, nature conservation.

In December 1983, Boun Somsy had a dream in which a beautiful woman, "dressed like a god," came to his simple house and told him to "go find a diamond." In his village of elephant hunters sixty kilometers from the southern Laotian city of Pakse, Boun interpreted her cryptic instructions as telling him to "go catch a white elephant."

The problem was that Boun, then thirty-nine, had never caught an elephant, which is a bit like telling a couch potato to go run a marathon.

Nevertheless, Boun instructed his wife to refrain from combing and oiling her hair, which would have made his hunting ropes slippery. Boum and his elephant-hunting friends slept rough in the forest in a simple shelter. On the fifth night of the hunt for the Lao equivalent of the Holy Grail, Boun had another dream. Same beautiful woman, similar message. "I will give you this mansion," she said, gesturing toward her estate. The next morning Boun spotted and captured a juvenile female elephant. On bringing the dirty animal back to the village and giving it a good scrub, he saw that it was "the color of old bamboo," a rare and holy white elephant.

Devotees, some from distant villages, came to pay homage to his white elephant, leaving behind offerings and some much-needed cash.

News of his special elephant spread and a Cambodian elephant trader offered him ten "normal" elephants for the white pachyderm. But before Boun could close the deal, a government official named Sali knocked on the door of his village house with the Laotian equivalent of "I'm from the government and I'm here to help you."

Sali and four white elephant examiners inspected the animal and gave Boun the good news that he would have the honor of donating the auspicious beast to the citizens of the fledgling People's Republic of Laos. In olden days the animal would have been offered to the king, but

Prince Souvanna Phouma, the nation's top-ranking royal, had been deposed as prime minister by Kaysone Phomvihane in 1975, making commoners Kaysone and his wife Thongvinh de facto royalty in the social hierarchy.

Boun was instructed to ride the people's elephant to the capital of Vientiane, a journey that took twenty-nine days.

He was offered neither compensation nor public gratitude.

The reason that Kaysone Phomvihane and his ethnic-Vietnamese wife Thongvinh wanted the white elephant is both completely understandable yet somehow paradoxical.

Here's the conundrum. The white elephant is seen as a religious miracle, a descendant of the holy white elephant that Queen Maya dreamt entered her body nine months before Prince Siddharta, who was to become Buddha, was born. The white elephant historically represents the power of the Buddhist kings of the region, and the kings of neighboring Burma, Thailand, and Cambodia fought a series of wars between 1549 and 1769 dedicated, in part, to stealing each other's white elephants. Kaysone Phomvihane (whose name derives from a Pali word describing the four sublime states of mind achieved by a Buddhist monk), the first prime minister, and later president, of communist Laos, simply wanted to be viewed as a fair, righteous, and powerful king.

Or, more likely, observers suggest, his wife Thongvinh Phomvihane wanted to be viewed as a fair, righteous, and powerful queen.

Through a well-placed Laotian friend I was given a rare interview with semi-reclusive Madame Thongvinh. Her husband was a Pathet Lao, a Vietnam-supported revolutionary hero – today his self-satisfied and well-fed portrait appears on the country's currency, and an eight-million-dollar museum has been built in his honor. To use an American simile, meeting Madame Thongvinh was like getting an interview with Martha Washington.

Looking like a frail seventy-something woman who had just woken from a nap, she was guarded and reticent. She wore a worn, not overly clean housedress. We sat in her comfortable house on the outskirts of Vientiane. She spoke neither French nor English, and my friend translated. After pleasantries on my part, greeted with stoic silence and the reluctant offering of a glass of water on hers, I asked about her white elephant.

"Why do you want to know?" she grunted, followed by a sailor-quality belch that threatened to wilt the plastic flowers in her living room, where most of the wall space was taken up by photos of her and her husband during their glory days, alongside one dramatic photo of her white elephant.

I EXPLAINED MY LONG INTEREST IN WHITE ELEPHANTS and desire to know more about white elephants in Lao culture.

Again she asked, "Why do you want to know?"

I tried another tack; implying that the white elephant

represented powerful leaders, I asked whether that was the reason her husband wanted the elephant.

"Where are you from?"

"America."

Her face seemed to freeze. Sure, I could have said Canada, but at times like this I get patriotic.

Her industrial-sized belch seemed even more vigorous.

The only moment of softness came when she explained how she loves animals and how she and her elephant are "soul partners" – when she is ill the elephant also feels ill, and vice versa. She told of her dreams that whenever she traveled overseas, the white elephant would be flying alongside her plane, protecting her.

I showed her the photo of Boun, the villager who captured her elephant. Madame Thongvinh snorted, said the elephant was sick while she was in Boun's care, and threw the photo back on my pile of papers, as if it was dirty.

Why was she so rude and unhelpful?

Pick a reason. She was tired and grumpy. She was not used to speaking with a foreigner. She doesn't like Americans. She was protective of the white elephant, which she considers "her property." She was afraid I would make fun of the richly symbolic animal. She had lost her power, position, and legacy, and the white elephant was the only symbol of the good old days that she had left. She just doesn't like to share her toys.

We had been given permission by the district authorities to visit her white elephant, and the next morning drove an hour and a half northwest to Phialat. En route, my Laotian friend called ahead to arrange lunch and was told that our white elephant viewing privileges had been revoked by Madame Thongvinh.

We went anyway and met one of the vets who over-sees the care of the animal.

He confirmed that the animal was indeed the personal property of Madame Thongvinh, and that her word in the district, her birthplace, was law. No, we couldn't see the elephant. Yes, the animal was healthy. Yes, Madame Thongvinh visits about twice a year; she is the only visitor. Yes, she and the elephant have a special relationship. Yes, she instructs that when the elephant is moved from one part of the buffer zone next to the national park to another, it is "camouflaged" with dark paint. No, we couldn't slip into the forest and search for it ourselves.

Laos's other white elephant, a male named Chaya-mongkhol (King of Elephants), died in 2010 at the Laos Zoo, making Madame Thongvinh's white elephant, which she's named Keo (Precious), the country's only such creature, the property of a woman who holds on to the idea that the animal will do for her what it has done for Buddhist rulers for centuries – show that she is a legi-timate, semi-divine leader. Perhaps the white elephant can compensate for her indignation at being kicked out of her executive position in the Communist Party for excessive corruption (allegedly smuggling heroin to Vietnam). Perhaps the animal can give a feeble old woman who has been sidelined by the younger generation (few people in

Vientiane know or care about her) one last glimmer of self-respect.

And Madame Thongvinh's elephant might be the last one for a while. While a photo of a wild white elephant, spotted in 1998 by a helicopter pilot, circulated in Lao conservation circles a few years ago, that animal has not been seen since. And the elephant population in Laos, which describes itself as the "Land of a Million Elephants" (and which featured Airavata, the archetypal white elephant, on its flag during the royalist period of 1952–1975), continues to crash. Khammoun Khounboline, an elephant conservation expert with conservation group WWF, estimates that there are only six hundred to eight hundred wild elephants left in the country, down from an estimated fifteen hundred to two thousand animals ten years ago.

And Boun, the man who had a dream and captured the animal?

After his epic elephant march to Vientiane to "donate" the elephant to the prime minister and his wife, Boun returned to his village broke and empty-handed. A few years later another government official came to his home with a gift, the only compensation or thanks he ever received. It is a painting on thin wood, about half as tall as he is, showing Boun's daughter, son-in-law, and granddaughter sitting on the white elephant that he captured through a mystical dream.

THE LONG (COSMOLOGICAL) MARCH OF THE WHITE ELEPHANT

How did white elephants become so powerful?

The white elephant mystique has its beginnings in animistic beliefs that were subsequently adopted and adapted by Hindu and Buddhist myth creators.

Animist, Hindu, and Buddhist deities, myths, and symbols have as much shared DNA as European royal families.

In ancient animistic pre-Hindu, pre-Buddhist times, the "normal" elephant was a potent village spirit because of its power, intelligence, and unpredictability. The rarely encountered white elephant was associated with rain clouds, a symbol of fertility.

It made sense for Hindu priests to build on this populist perception, and elephants were introduced into Hindu mythology. Four-tusked Airavata, who rose to the surface when the celestial Sea of Milk was churned, was an elephant Adam and begat all the elephants that followed. Just as sun-eagle Garuda became the mount of Hindu god Vishnu, the white elephant Airavata (Erawan in Thai) became the steed of Indra, the Hindu god of the heavens. Airavata is said to have boasted: "Of lordly elephants I am Airavata, and among men I am the monarch."

(In parallel, the early Hindu proselytizers, faced with villagers unwilling to give up their animistic beliefs, took a "normal" elephant's head, stuck it on the son of top-of-the-line gods Shiva and his consort Parvati, and created Ganesha, easily the most popular of all current Hindu deities.)

Buddhist teachers built on the already deep-rooted Hindu beliefs of people they wanted to convert. The Hindu elephant god Airavata, the Buddhist teachers argued, was actually an incarnate Buddha (bodhisattva). But raising the stakes even higher, they declared that a holy white elephant appeared in a dream to Lord Buddha's mother-to-be, Maya. The white elephant, holding a white lotus flower (the female symbol) in his silvery trunk, uttered a long, drawn-out cry, bowed three times, and touched his forehead to the floor. Then he gently struck Maya's right side and entered her womb. The Queen reported this extraordinary vision to the court astrologers, who divined that she would give birth to a great king or a great seer. Nine months later, Prince Siddhartha was born, the Buddhist equivalent of a virgin birth. Present at the birth was Indra, offering his hair as a gift.

And the connection with the Buddhist kings?

One needs only look at the symbolism surrounding King Bhumibol Adulyadej of Thailand, the world's longest reigning monarch (and owner of eleven white elephants, arguably the most ever of any Buddhist king). He is a much-loved man whom many consider to be semi-divine. He is referred to as Rama IX, and the use of the name "Rama" clearly positions him as an avatar of Vishnu, thereby linking him with both Rama (of Ramayana fame) who was the seventh avatar of Vishnu and with Buddha, who was Vishnu's ninth avatar. To consolidate the symbolism, King Bhumibol's royal emblem features Garuda (*Krut* in Thai), which is Vishnu's mount. When one sees the Thai *Krut* on a government building, it signifies that it is under the protection and control of the Vishnu-related king, literally "the king/Vishnu is in the building." So, following the circuitous but pervasive logic of Hindu-Buddhist belief systems, King Bhumibol (and other Buddhist kings) are related to the most powerful Hindu gods, who themselves are also closely associated with Buddha. The white elephant, which adorned Thailand's flag from 1855 to 1916, is a symbol of that cosmic power, and in the context of Asian Buddhist power-grabs, the monarch with the most white elephants wins.

Like any religious symbol, particularly one that represents a god-king, a visitor is advised not to belittle the divine animal. An entertainment called Wilson's English Circus visited Bangkok in the late nineteenth century and drew a huge crowd by advertising that a real white elephant would participate in the next performance. According to Norwegian traveler Carl Bock, "two clowns came in and began jesting about the white elephant. Then in came a small Indian elephant, appearing as white as snow; not a dark spot could be seen anywhere. But the elephant left white marks on everything he touched. He was chalked all over, and when one of the clowns told the other to 'rub his nose against the elephant and he will leave his mark on you,' an ominous silence was maintained by the great mass of the people, only broken here and there by a suppressed titter." The Thais were naturally annoyed that fun was being made of an incarnated Buddha. In the usual Thai way of avoiding open criticism, they merely expressed their confident belief that Wilson would be punished for his disrespect of the Lord Buddha. Several days after the Bangkok fiasco, the impostor elephant died at sea on a trip to Singapore. The too-clever Mr. Wilson suffered from dysentery during the voyage and died almost immediately on landing. The reputation of the true white elephant remained untarnished.

"IT'S A WHITE ELEPHANT." "NO IT ISN'T." "IS SO."

The problem is that white elephants are rarely white, and it can often be difficult for laymen to tell at a glance that they are viewing a manifestation of Lord Buddha. What distinguishes a normal elephant from a sacred white elephant?

Jeffrey A. McNeely, chief scientist of the World Conservation Union and co-author of *Mammals of Thailand*, points out that unusual coloring is just one aspect of white elephantness. Most white elephant adjudicators agree that in order for a white elephant to be kosher, it has to have four toenails instead of the normal five (and they should be white), the tail and trunk should be straight and long, the eyes must be pearl-colored with yellow irises enclosed by red rings, and the skin must turn red, rather than becoming darker, after having water poured on it.

Savet Dhanapradit, a member of Thailand's White Elephant Selection Committee, remembers the complications of his first charge, in the late 1950s:

> We received word at the palace that there was a miraculous elephant at a village near the town of Yala. People who drank water from its trunk were cured of their ills ... But the elephant wasn't perfect ... not so beautiful, but it was very intelligent and mixed well with people. My only objection was that her toenails were not suitable. My bosses and I argued for a month about that animal. In the end I concurred with my superiors and signed the certificate [making the animal a *chang*

sam-khan]. Dhanapradit says that even the Royal Stable's top current white elephant, considered the finest beast in generations, is only "80% perfect."

While these deliberations can take on the atmosphere of "how many angels can dance on the head of a pin," there is one rarely observed characteristic that guarantees a fast track to white elephant status. Some ancient texts decreed that a sleeping white elephant must not snore but should emit the gentle sounds of Burmese and Thai classical musical instruments.

Tourists (not the author or his wife) mess around with guns at a Phnom Penh shooting range.

Photo: Aaron Bradford

UZI FEVER

Releasing the macho urges with a bang in Cambodia.

PHNOM PENH, CAMBODIA

here are plenty of reasons not to shoot guns in Cambodia. The country suffered almost unimaginable cruelties and mass murder during the Khmer Rouge period – one out of every four citizens was killed. Globally, terrorists wield guns that strike down innocent people. We in the West retaliate with our own brand of deadly warfare. In the United States we read almost daily about idiots with easy access to guns who kill other people.

But here's the politically incorrect reality, for me at least. Shooting a gun, at targets and under benign conditions, is sort of fun.

In Cambodia's capital Phnom Penh, Taiwanese entrepreneur Victor Chao has set up one of the country's two public shooting ranges a few minutes from Phnom Penh airport and around the corner from a new golf course. Since 1996 he's invested some $900,000 in the forty-five bay, five-hectare facility that he has named the Marksmen Club-Eagle Force Headquarters.

Chao, 48, showed me the weapons I could shoot. Uzis

and M16s, Smith and Wesson pistols, and Al Capone-like machine guns. You rent your gun of choice and pay for ammo.

"Let's start with this baby," I said, hefting a Dragonov, a Russian sniper rifle. My voice took on a Sylvester Stallone-like quality.

"That's not a good shirt, is it?"

"Powder marks?"

Chao nodded. "Tough to get out."

"Okay Victor, show me how this thing works."

Zap, bam, wham. Getting into the groove, I reached for a London Scorpion, a Cold War-era, British-designed .32 pistol with a folding stock, later manufactured by the Czechs for special forces worldwide. I felt mildly James Bondish.

So, what's the attraction?

Social analyst Dave Barry put it like this:

"Women often ask, 'what do men REALLY want, deep in their souls?' The best answer," he said, "based on in-depth analysis of the complex and subtle interplay of thought, instinct, and emotion that constitutes the male psyche, is that deep in their souls, men want to watch stuff go 'bang.'"

Barry was talking about Car Bowling, in which low-flying pilots drop bowling balls on cars parked on the runways of (hopefully) little-used private airstrips.

Now I've never had the pleasure of playing Car Bowling, but I've always had a hankering to play Rambo. Not for real, you understand. Just enough to smell the gunpowder and ruin my hearing for a day.

"Is it true that when you rent the grenade launcher you get a cow to shoot at?" I asked.

"Ah, I've heard that story as well," Chao replied. "But I don't do that. If you want to shoot a grenade into a cow, you'll have to go to Phnom Penh's *other* shooting range. It's run by the military."

"Then let me try the Glock."

Is this joy at making loud noises at all Freudian? Maybe. Does this have a redeeming social value? Come on, this is guy talk. Shooting ranges are popular around the world. Chao got the idea for his facility after visiting popular legal shooting ranges in Hawaii.

Did it make me want to commit public mayhem? Not at all, but that's a fear of Cambodia's officials who threaten to close the Marksmen Club-Eagle Force Headquarters, which hosts some six thousand customers annually. Writing in the *Cambodia Daily*, Chao defended his operation. "Kidnappers are not among our customers," he wrote. "Our customers are tourists, businessmen, fairly wealthy people who are actually victims of crime."

I invited my wife Monique to have a go. Chao nodded approval. "Women shoot better than men," he said. "Men are too busy pretending they're John Wayne and Clint Eastwood to shoot straight. Women just focus on the task."

I offered Monique the AK-47.

"Not interested," she said.

"Come on," I urged. "You'll regret it if you don't."

To please me (or shut me up) she gingerly hoisted the weapon, fired one shot, and carefully put it down.

"That's it?" I asked.

"One's enough," she said. "Can we have lunch now?"

A captive civet in Vietnam being fed coffee cherries.

YOU KNOW WHERE THAT COFFEE'S BEEN?

Searching for the perfect dung-delicious civet coffee.

BUON MA THUOT, VIETNAM

ysters. Termites. Camembert. Snake blood. Brains. Broccoli.

On the long list of strange things people voluntarily ingest, one might add civet coffee.

Civet coffee, called *café chon* in Vietnam and *kopi luwak* in Indonesia, is probably the only popular foodstuff that is consumed by people simply because it has passed through the digestive system of a wild animal.

It is also one of the world's most expensive delicacies; in 2008 upscale John Lewis department store in London made the evening "you'll-love-this-next-story" newscasts when it charged $100 for a cup of the brew.

I went to Vietnam and Indonesia to taste civet coffee, made moderately well known when it appeared on Jack Nicholson's and Morgan Freeman's "bucket list" in the movie of the same name.

My journey isn't all that strange, actually.

First, I love coffee, and admit to being a coffee snob. I never drink dishwater American coffee but relish a strong, small Italian espresso, straight up, no milk or sugar, always in a ceramic cup, never in paper or plastic.

Second, I like to eat strange things and am not squeamish. I'm not a gurgitator in the sense of Takeru Kobayashi or Joey Chestnut or Sonya Thomas, folks who compete to see who can eat the most of something in a limited period of time. I'm a selective ingester who enjoys experimenting. That has led me to enjoy foie gras, frogs, and horse in France and chewy goat testicles in Java. Python, eaten in Borneo, tastes a bit like chicken, crocodile tastes like turtle, fermented Mongolian mare's milk called *kumis* tastes simply horrible. In Sulawesi, dog is gamy and fruit bat is like honey-marinated wild boar. And *balut* in the Philippines, a duck-egg with embryo, is completely yucky but said to help male potency. I've tucked into monkey in the Central African Republic; ants in Laos; beetles, grasshoppers, and scorpions in Thailand. In Vietnam my son and I ploughed through a nine-course cobra meal, which included the heart, blood, skin, flesh, and penis.

Civet coffee would be a piece of cake.

Except.

Except I was fully aware of the method by which civet coffee is produced.

THE LIFE CYCLE OF THIS BEVERAGE IS THE EASY TARGET of sophomoric body-waste jokes.

Start with the wild Asian palm civet, *Paradoxurus hermaphroditus*, a fairly common, attractive, raccoon-like, omnivorous, cat-sized animal with a pointy snout and a bushy tail.

The civet (sometimes mistakenly described as a weasel and often incorrectly called a cat) likes the taste of ripe coffee berries, the cherry-sized fruit that contains the seed — what we call the coffee bean. According to the legend, which has almost certainly been enhanced by the marketing departments of the numerous companies producing civet coffee, the civet only selects the ripest, juiciest fruits. The critter nibbles away the coffee-berry flesh (which tastes vaguely like cherries, actually) and swallows the seed. Then the gustatory transformation takes place — the civet's digestive enzymes impart a rich, chocolaty essence to the coffee while softening the hard edges. A day later the flavor-enhanced seeds emerge as civet-coffee feces, shaped like a skinny pine cone and resembling a roughly made peanut-coated chocolate bar. The seeds are collected, cleaned, roasted, and sold for ridiculous amounts of money.

The resulting brew is said to taste terrific.

I WAS INVITED TO TRY CIVET COFFEE IN THE MIDDLE-class home of Mai Van Kien, in the town of Buon Ma Thuot in the Central Highlands of Vietnam. Kien, a coffee trader and farmer, is one of the happiest and most vigorous eighty-year-olds I've met. "This will taste great," he suggested, pouring hot water into the ubiquitous Vietnamese coffee filter device that has been likened to a "top hat" and technically described as a "tin coffee thingy."

I tasted a brew that was strong, earthy, flavorful, nutty, and round. Kien, who fought with South Vietnamese forces in what in Vietnam is called "the American war," was imprisoned by the North Vietnamese victors for a year after the conflict for re-education. Today he is at peace and sat with Nguyen Thi My, his seventy-something wife, laughing and never moving far from each other, one of the happiest and most touchy-feely couples I've seen. His house was filled with well-tended potted plants, framed family photos, an aquarium, and a big TV. On the front porch, next to coffee drying on the ground, stood a motorcycle. His secret for his "wealthy life?" "Loyal marriage, eat lots of vegetables, get to sleep on time, be careful." Coffee didn't fit into his recipe for happiness though; when I visited, Kien and his wife drank tea.

But the problem with drinking coffee with Kien is that small-scale coffee producers like him, as well as the big Vietnamese manufacturers, regularly add flavorings to their coffee. Was that chocolate essence I tasted the result of the civet's gut juices working their magic or was it added by the person roasting the beans over a cocoa-wood fire? What about the slight buttery aftertaste? The peppery tang? The sweetness – natural or a touch of sugar? And is that a hint of red wine?

Some large Vietnamese coffee factories go beyond

flavoring and have become civet coffee alchemists. Huge Vietnamese coffee company Trung Nguyen manufactures an artificially enhanced brew they describe as "produced by an enzyme treatment process that mimics the changes produced in the coffee beans by the civet and which releases a whole spectrum of flavors that normally lie dormant." Their "weasel-enzyme" technique is secret and has the benefit, Ma Son Tung, the company's market development manager notes, "of not requiring any involvement from the animals."

AND THAT'S THE PROBLEM I FACED. LOTS OF PEOPLE will offer you civet coffee. Is it genuine? Has it been enhanced? But faux civet coffee wasn't my goal. I sought the real deal. I needed a control sample, a somewhat-scientific taste test in which I could compare civet coffee with "normal" coffee made with beans from the same plantation, with both samples prepared in the same way. A double-blind experiment.

I asked my friend Dang Xuan Vu for help.

Dang Xuan Vu was my guide during my search for the last elephant hunter in Vietnam, tolerating my quirks and answering endless questions. He understood my dilemma with tasting civet coffee in isolation. The brew might taste sweet, soft, round, full, chocolatey, or a hundred other wine-like adjectives. But is it sweeter, softer, rounder, fuller, and chocolatier than normally produced coffee that has never seen the inside of a civet's gut?

Vu, whose family owns a three-and-a-half hectare coffee plantation in Vietnam's Central Highlands, mailed me two vacuum-sealed packets of coffee. The first was "normal" Robusta, the cheap rustic coffee grown locally. The second, roasted and ground in exactly the same way, was Robusta civet coffee.

I prepared both samples the same way, in a French press, and served the coffee to guests at a dinner party in Bangkok. Almost unanimously, my friends and I preferred the civet coffee, using phrases like "rounder," "sweeter," and "drinkable" to describe the taste. That doesn't mean they would have preferred civet coffee to, say, an Illy espresso, but they did prefer civet coffee to the "normal" brew.

WHILE I WAS IMBIBING CIVET COFFEE, I HAD A NAGGING question.

Who was the first person to have the audacity to go to the trouble of making and drinking civet coffee?

None of the farmers I spoke with in Vietnam or Indonesia could cite long-standing cultural use of civet coffee. Dang Xuan Vu, whose family has grown coffee for generations, said "yes, the old folks said that weasel coffee is the best, but up until recently we had never tried it." Some farmers say *café chon* is excretory ecstasy; other farmers won't touch the stuff, reflecting the view of a farmer I met in Vietnam who disdains it because it's "made from poo."

Dang Xuan Vu has a plausible explanation. He suggests French or Dutch colonial plantation owners forbade their Vietnamese and Indonesian workers from drinking the valuable coffee they harvested, so the poor farmers had no option but to clean and roast the unwanted feces-enrobed beans that had been excreted by the civet. Word got back to the European masters that this was a good brew and then the marketing folks took over.

But still, who might have been Civet Coffee Drinker One? Was he or she a lateral-thinking peasant hero who genuinely bought into the idea that civets only select the finest coffee berries? Or just some desperate, curious, anti-establishment goof-off who said "what the hell?"

Of course there's a lot of cultural relativism in considering what constitutes acceptable food. The French eat horse while Americans never touch the stuff. Many Europeans relish fresh oysters; many Asians gag at the slimy mollusk. Lots of Southeast Asians love sticky and stinky durian, while Westerners won't approach a fruit that smells like eating strawberries and cream in a badly maintained public toilet. Is it texture? Taste? A cultural concept of what food *is*?

My self-inflicted food prohibitions are based less on taste appeal and more on conservation right-mindedness. I try to boycott Chinese restaurants that serve shark's fin and coral reef fish. I've refused to eat bear. Chimpanzee is a no-no. Birds' nests though, made from the saliva of swiftlets, is okay (but tasteless).

I find people's illogical fears of all kinds fascinating.

One friend hates crowds. Another hates solitude. My wife can pretty much deal with house mice, but gets goofy when confronted by a spider or snake.

I don't know why I'm relatively immune to funny foods. Actually, I'm relatively immune to many fears. I can speak in public, climb tall towers, hike on rocky ledges, scuba dive, rescue a mouse from our cat's grasp, and liberate spiders with nary a concern. Yet in a restaurant I prefer to sit with my back against the wall.

CIVETS HAVE THEIR OWN PROBLEMS – CIVET COFFEE might disappear because the civets themselves are disappearing.

The Asian palm civet, while commonly found in forests and rural areas in South and Southeast Asia, is a protected species in Vietnam. The animal is becoming scarce in some areas, ironically a victim of farmers cutting down forests to plant coffee. The other problem is that civets are pests and eat chickens and ducks, so farmers often have little compunction about shooting the critters. There's an animal rights issue too – wild civet dung is awfully hard to find and Indonesian and Vietnamese entrepreneurs keep wild-caught civets in cramped and dirty cages, force-feeding them coffee cherries. And the *coup de civet* is that the flesh tastes pretty good. It is said to be terrific when roasted by farmers in a thatched-roof farmhouse. And it is said to be even better when fried with garlic and lemongrass at the Binh Minh restaurant in

Dak Mil, some seventy kilometers outside Buon Ma Thuot, in the heart of the Central Highlands coffee-growing region. The owner, a taciturn Chinese-Vietnamese businessman, admitted he fries several dozen animals a week. But he clammed up when we asked too many questions – after all, civets are protected in Vietnam and he fully realizes his business is illegal. Nevertheless, civet's on the menu, costing roughly seven times that of pork, selling for about five dollars per plate.

I MANAGED TWO BLIND TASTINGS.

The first, in Ho Chi Minh City, was put together by friends in the coffee business, with Arabica coffee from the same Central Highlands farm, the only difference being one sample was *café chon*, the other was "normal" coffee. Both were roasted and prepared in the same way.

I found it easy to distinguish between the two samples, with the *café chon* being richer in flavor and less stringent.

For an even more sophisticated tasting, I flew to Medan, North Sumatra, a dingy, ramshackle city of two million that hadn't changed much in the thirty years since I had first visited. Half an hour out of town I was welcomed to the head office of P.T. Coffindo, which prides itself as providing *kopi luwak* made only from wild civets who live in the coffee plantations, not in cages.

They agreed to set up a comparative tasting of *kopi luwak* (which in Indonesian means "coffee-civet") and "normal" coffee.

Herry Setiawan is a certified coffee taster working with Coffindo; one diploma hanging on the wall of his glass-enclosed tasting room identifies him as a "star cupper," which means he is qualified to judge international coffee competitions. Like his counterparts in the fields of wine and chocolate production, his palate and sense of smell are highly sensitive organs.

Using jargon reminiscent of wine tasting, Setiawan suggested I pay attention to "body, acidity, sweetness, flavor, color, and aroma."

Setiawan set out several small bowls, half filled with normal coffee, half with *kopi luwak*. All the samples were high-quality Arabica from the same plantation in Aceh, North Sumatra.

First we examined and sniffed the dry coffee that Herry Setiawan had just roasted and ground. Already I could detect a difference – the normal coffee was earthy, with an after-the-rain freshness. The *kopi luwak*, on the other hand, had distinct notes of dark chocolate, caramel, and something I couldn't quite identify. "Forest flowers?" Setiawan suggested.

He then added mineral water that had boiled and cooled to 93°C – he was very specific about the tem-perature. Setiawan slowly stirred the brew and sniffed the back of the spoon. The aroma was enhanced by the addition of hot water, and in the *kopi luwak* I smelled a note of something unexpected. "Green tea?" I asked. "Good nose," Setiawan said.

Then came the tasting. Setiawan showed me how to half fill the spoon, loudly slurp it into the mouth with a good intake of air, swish it around the tongue, and spit it into a red plastic pail. The two samples were brewed weak as dishwater and undrinkable as beverages. Yet I could taste that the normal coffee was nutty, grassy, and "green." The *kopi luwak*, on the other hand, was rounder, with distinct notes of milk chocolate, caramel, and the flowers I had smelled earlier.

Although *kopi luwak* and café chon account for a small percentage of coffee production in Indonesia and Vietnam, the markups are phenomenal. P.T. Coffindo sells a kilogram of roasted kopi luwak beans for around $800, about forty times the price of their "normal" Arabica. But the market is getting crowded and I'm curious how much demand there really is. Maybe the marketing folks should be more adventurous with their branding — I wonder whether a product called "Excretory Ecstasy" or "Fecal Fabulous" or "Dung Delicious" would boost sales.

I'll continue to search for the perfect fecalicious *kopi luwak*. But sometimes I feel the need to expand my gustatory horizons and take on new challenges. My Australian friends swear that I'll love Vegemite.

ELEPHANT DUNG COFFEE –
THE NEXT BIG THING?

For a bigger hit, coffee lovers can try Black Ivory Coffee, made with the help of elephants and produced in much the same way as civet coffee. Blake Dinkin, a Canadian entrepreneur who has spent $300,000 developing the concept, says, "When an elephant eats coffee, its stomach acid breaks down the protein found in coffee, which is a key factor in bitterness. You end up with a cup that's very smooth."

Dinkin says that during the fifteen to thirty hours it takes the animal to digest the beans, the coffee cherries ferment and stew together with bananas, sugar cane, and other ingredients to infuse earthy and fruity flavors. He describes the taste as "full-bodied, with hints of ripe red cherries, chocolate, and a hint of grass."

The coffee is produced by rescued animals at the Golden Triangle Asian Elephant Foundation in northern Thailand, which earns eight percent of the coffee's total sales. That income can add up, since the cleaned, sun-dried, and roasted beans sell for about $1,100 per kilogram; a four-espresso-cup serving can cost around $40 in luxury hotels in Thailand and the Maldives. One reason for the high cost: the elephants aren't efficient coffee producers – it takes thirty-three kilograms of raw coffee cherries to produce one kilogram of Black Ivory coffee, Dinkin says. Elephants are an inefficient production machine, he adds. "The majority of beans get chewed up, broken, or lost in tall grass after being excreted."

The smile is the trickiest bit.

MONA LISA ON MY MIND

Vietnamese artists search for that enigmatic smile.

HO CHI MINH CITY, VIETNAM

She has many identities and genders.
She was kidnapped, maybe by Picasso.
She lived in the Palace of Versailles.
She spent time in Bonaparte's bedroom.
Nat King Cole, Cole Porter, Santana, Bob Dylan,
and Britney Spears sang about her.
She appeared twice in The Simpsons.
She has no eyebrows or eyelashes.

he is the world's most famous painting. Created by Leonardo da Vinci in the early sixteenth century, the *Mona Lisa* (called *La Gioconda* in Italian and *La Joconde* in French) has been subject to the highest form of flattery – painters the world over have copied her likeness.

And Ground Zero for *Mona Lisa* copies is Vietnam. In the hothouse commercial atmosphere of Ho Chi Minh City and, to a lesser extent, Hanoi, Vietnam's artists churn out hundreds, perhaps thousands, of *Mona Lisa* paintings a year.

Kha Huen, a soft-faced twenty-nine-year-old artist in Ho Chi Minh City, takes about three days to paint a *Mona Lisa*. "I can do a Monet, Dalí, or Van Gogh in one day," he says over soft drinks at a café, "but the *Mona Lisa* has more details." Working as an in-house artist at a downtown art shop, Kha paints about thirty *Mona Lisa*s a year, which sell for around fifty dollars. There are perhaps a hundred painters in Ho Chi Minh City creating *Mona Lisa*s, he estimates.

Visitors to downtown Ho Chi Minh City can hardly walk fifty meters without passing in front of an art shop. On the walls hang copy paintings of Botero's fat people with small heads, Warhol's Marilyn, Van Gogh's sunflowers, and Dalí's melted watches. Like "copy-watches" and "copy-golf shirts," "copy-paintings" seem to be just another commodity to be sold in this overheated economy. But while the latest Hollywood movie or Swiss watch is protected by copyright and trademark regulations, a painting by da Vinci is free game.

> *Few pieces of art have been the subject of so much artsy analysis. For example, Professor Margaret Livingstone of Harvard University used the* Mona Lisa *smile to illustrate her theory that the human eye uses two types of vision, foveal (or direct vision, which is good for detail) and peripheral. "The elusive quality of the* Mona Lisa's *smile can be explained by the fact that her smile is almost entirely in low spatial frequencies," Livingstone said, "and so is seen best by your peripheral vision."*

Like most copy-artists in Ho Chi Minh City, Vy Vi spends his days in the middle of a small shop, sitting on a low stool in front of an easel, copying works of Klimt and Hooper. When he gets lucky a businessman will walk in, set down a photograph of his kids, and ask for a painted portrait that is as close to the original as possible. There's not much request for creative license in this business. Vy Vi explains that his *Mona Lisa* usually requires six days, but he sometimes feels uneasy working on the famous face. "It's so well known that people will see if I make a mistake," he says. He paints some twenty *Mona Lisa*s a year, which cost $43, about the standard price throughout the country.

Some of the Vietnamese *Mona Lisa*s are excellent. Some are clearly "just off" in some way – either the color is wrong or the background is too sharp or too soft, or the details on her dress too ornate, or her smile a bit, well, just not right.

The famous *Mona Lisa* smile is the trickiest thing to get right, Vu Dan Thang, a Hanoi-based artist says.

The question of what lies behind her half-smile has spurred debate for centuries. Who was she? What secrets does she keep?

Art historians have speculated that she is Lisa Gherardini, wife of the Florentine cloth merchant Francesco del Giocondo. But there are other theories: She is Leonardo's secret mistress. She is pregnant. She is an aristocratic lady with her own private secrets. She is following Leonardo's mischievous instruction to project an enigmatic image. Sigmund Freud thought she was a remembrance of Leonardo's mother. Italian art historian Angelo Paratico goes a step further, speculating that she is actually a Chinese slave who was Leonardo's mother – according to Paratico there are several proofs of da Vinci's Chinese ancestry, "For instance, the fact he was writing with his left hand from left to right … and he was also a vegetarian, which was not common [among Europeans]." Others speculate that she is Leonardo's male assistant and lover. That she is Leonardo himself, in drag.

The Vietnamese artists I met acknowledged that they are simply copying art, and trying to do so in an artistically valid way.

So where's the line between copy-art and fake?

Michelangelo was found guilty of forging a marble sculpture of Cupid for his patron, Lorenzo di Cosimo de Medici, rubbing his newly wrought work with soil before passing it off as an antiquity. Picasso was also thought to have signed off on a painting that wasn't done by him.

Thomas Hoving, former director of New York City's Metropolitan Museum of Art, estimates that as much as forty percent of art in the market today is either a "half-forgery," meaning genuinely old works that have been altered to be attributed to a more valuable style or artist, or outright fakes.

Obviously, none of the Vietnam street paintings would ever be confused with the priceless masterpiece hanging in the Louvre. But an artist takes pride in his work, and I wondered how satisfying is it to copy *Mona Lisa*, day in, day out.

"It's challenging," Doan Le Quang, a Hanoi-based artist said. "But I'd rather do my own thing." I ask if I could see some of his paintings. He sifts among the Gauguins and Magrittes and Renoirs and pulls out a few idyllic landscapes of Vietnamese countryside scenes. They are attractive, although not to my taste. Does his shop sell a lot of these scenes of water buffalo and rice fields, thatched-roof houses and temples? "A few," he says shyly. "But not as many as these," he admits, pointing to a Klimt's *Woman in Gold* and Monet's *Waterlilies*.

Pretty fun job, except when
President Clinton comes to lunch.

INTO THE FRYING PAN

Vietnam's street kids learn the restaurant business.

HANOI, VIETNAM

"Postcards, mister?"

I explained to the teenaged boy outside a luxury hotel in Hanoi that I didn't need any more postcards.

"Please mister."

So I bought a few more postcards, hoping my dollar would buy the young man a meal or two.

Officially, there are some nineteen thousand street children in Hanoi, but social workers estimate the number of destitute youngsters at twice that number. Most of these children and teenagers have no support system and scrape out a hard-scrabble living flogging trinkets. Some turn to drugs, crime, or prostitution.

A lucky few get accepted to KOTO, an imaginative program that trains street kids in restaurant-related skills.

So I did my bit for youth empowerment by eating a tasty lunch of prawn tofu crêpe, fresh mango juice, and banana coconut rum cake (about $6.50 for the lot) at the eighty-seat KOTO Café, adjacent to Hanoi's famous Temple of Literature.

KOTO, WHICH STANDS FOR KNOW ONE TEACH ONE, was created by Jimmy Pham, a Vietnamese-born, naturalized Australian who decided to do something for street kids that would be longer lasting than buying them a few bowls of noodles and some clothes. He established KOTO in 1996 to train young men and women as chefs and restaurant managers, skills that are much in demand in booming Vietnam.

I spoke with KOTO graduate Do Van Kiem, a bright-eyed man with neatly parted hair who now works as a bartender at the elegant Sofitel Metropole in Hanoi.

Kiem, now twenty-two, explained that four years ago he had shined Jimmy Pham's shoes. Pham asked Kiem about his life and heard a story that was touching, but perhaps not all that unusual. Kiem had arrived in Hanoi from Ha Nam province when he was thirteen. His family were farmers ("it was a boring existence," he recalls) and he sought a better life. But things weren't easy once he got to Hanoi – in the capital he slept rough, was arrested for being a street peddler, and sometimes went ten days without earning a single dong.

Jimmy Pham listened to Kiem's tale with a sense of recognition and empathy. Pham's family had fled the war zone of Vietnam in 1974. They escaped initially to

Singapore, then were shunted to Saudi Arabia and eventually settled in Australia. After completing high school, Pham worked at a variety of odd jobs – from making *sangas* at an all-night sandwich shop in Kings Cross to selling vacuum cleaners door to door. It was a tough upbringing for Jimmy and his four siblings, as Jimmy's mother, on her own at that time, struggled to bring up her family in a new country. But it wasn't as tough a life as the situation for kids like Kiem.

Pham enrolled in a travel and tourism course and returned to Vietnam in the early 1990s as a tour guide. He spoke enough Vietnamese to be able to understand the harrowing stories of the street kids in Saigon.

Pham fed them, bought them clothes, and paid for them to attend school. But perhaps most important, he listened as the kids explained that if they were ever going to get off the streets, they needed to learn a trade.

Kiem graduated from KOTO in 2002. He remembers the date, March 18. Like all the KOTO graduates, he was immediately offered a job, he explains, as we sit at a table in the luxurious garden of the Sofitel. "I'm lucky to be working here."

NADINE ZIEGELDORF, CHIEF EXECUTIVE OFFICER OF THE project, took me to the KOTO training center and described the eighteen-month training program, developed by Melbourne's Boxhill Institute. There is practical training to be sure, but perhaps equally important is that the students – some one hundred of them by 2004 – are provided with a sense of family and responsibility. They earn salaries, are given loans to buy bicycles, and look after one another.

AFTER LUNCH I STOPPED BY THE KITCHEN. SOME TWELVE young women and men were busy slicing, frying, steaming, and hustling to prepare lunch for a restaurant full of curious and hungry folks – a combination of tourists and ex-patriates working in Hanoi. Half the kitchen staff wore the white uniforms of trainees, half wore the blue uniforms of KOTO graduates who were employed full-time by the restaurant.

The cooks were busy, but without interrupting their work managed to smile for a quick photo. I tried to imagine the scene in 2001 when the restaurant was given three-hours notice that former U.S. President Bill Clinton, and his one hundred thirty-strong entourage, was going to have lunch at KOTO. As an added challenge, the VIP group had to be fed during the twenty-five minutes allotted in their tight schedule. Clinton asked his trainee waiter, eighteen-year-old Phung Van Hai, what was good. The president, known for his love affair with food, or-dered grilled vegetables and hummus in a baguette, washed down with a banana milkshake, a café latte, and a Diet Coke. Clinton left satisfied; Phung Van Hai now has a steady job at the Hanoi Sheraton.

FEEL-GOOD FOOD EXPLOSION

Since I first wrote this story, KOTO has spawned a mini-wave of efforts to develop similarly helpful training programs.

In Vietnam, where KOTO originated, a group called Streets International has created a "teaching" restaurant in the old city of Hoi An, aimed, like KOTO, at getting kids off the street and into respectable, paying jobs. The students undergo the same eighteen-month training as students at the Institute of Culinary Education in Manhattan.

Efforts in Laos include Makphet in Vientiane, run by Friends International.

But it's in Cambodia that the feel-good restaurant movement has been most active. Many of these visitor-friendly restaurants and training centers are in the tourist city of Siem Reap, near the Angkor Wat temple complex, others are in the capital, Phnom Penh. One of the largest is Friends the Restaurant, part of the TREE global alliance of training restaurants; a quick Internet search will indicate many others worthy of a visit.

A golfer in the 1950s (and his caddie) playing on
the rough Dalat Palace Golf Course.

NAPALM BE GONE

The king, the architect, and the scoundrel
who created Vietnam's golf boom.

DALAT, VIETNAM

uccess has many fathers. Golf is flourishing in Vietnam, and the wave can be traced to a puppet king, a French architect who restored Roman ruins, and a rich American who craved virgins.

I SPENT PART OF THE VIETNAM WAR-PERIOD PROTESTING it, along with my fellow high-minded and moderately spoiled American university student friends. Then, after we got rid of Lyndon Johnson only to watch Bobby Kennedy get shot and Richard Nixon elected, I entered the United States Peace Corps, which at that time offered a deferment to the conflict we considered unjust and "not our problem."

I was assigned to Sarawak, a Malaysian state on the island of Borneo. Just a short hop across the South China Sea from Vietnam, as it turned out.

During those heady, full-of-life days I never thought that I would eventually love the sport of golf or go to Vietnam to play it.

It has become a travel writer's cliché to point out the irony that the Ho Chi Minh Trail, which Americans tried so hard to napalm into oblivion (the Vietnamese refer to the conflict as the "American War"), has now been renamed the Ho Chi Minh Golf Trail and features courses that would not be out of place in such high-ticket golf destinations as Hawaii, Spain, or nearby Thailand.

According to Nguyen Ngoc Chu, general secretary of the fledgling Vietnam Golf Association, Vietnam currently has seventeen golf courses, about the same as Singapore, which has eighteen. But thirty more courses are under construction in Vietnam, he says, while more than fifty additional ones are in the planning stages. That would give the country some one hundred courses, about half the number of golf behemoths like Thailand and Indonesia.

Recognizing this growth and the quality of the courses at their December 2007 meeting in Cancun, Mexico, the International Association of Golf Tour Operators designated Vietnam as the "undiscovered golf destination of the year."

What's the reason for this boom?

Vietnam's strong economy has created a middle class that loves the game, and tourism numbers are robust. The

World Travel and Tourism Council (WTTC) predicts that Vietnam will be among the top ten tourist destinations in the world by 2016.

MY FAVORITE GOLF COURSE IN VIETNAM IS THE DALAT Palace in the hill resort of the same name in the Central Highlands. It's also the oldest, and the presence and success of the Dalat course set the stage for all the courses that followed.

It was at Dalat that puppet king Bao Dai, a famous French architect named Ernest Hébrard, and an absurdly rich, reclusive scoundrel (with a penchant for deflowering virgins) named Larry Hillblom played roles in building Vietnam's golf industry.

IT STARTED WITH BAO DAI, THE LAST OF THE NUYEN kings. French-educated and widely seen as serving French, and later Japanese, interests, he encouraged construction of the course.

The golf course was part of Bao Dai's master plan to design Dalat town. A cynical observer might conclude that Bao Dai was pressured to create a town in the cool hills of Dalat, altitude fifteen hundred meters, by French bureaucrats who sweltered in the miasma of Saigon.

That may be, but the selection of Ernest Hébrard as senior architect was an inspired choice. His credentials included the redesign of the Greek city of Thessaloniki, Greece, after the Great Fire of 1917, the upgrading of Casablanca, and the restoration of Diocletian's palace at Split in Croatia. In 1922 Hébrard modified his master plan by allotting space on Doi Cu Hill for a golf course. Not coincidentally, the course was near the luxurious Dalat Palace Hotel, then and now the town's architectural and touristic landmark.

FOLLOWING ITS CONSTRUCTION, NOBODY HAD MUCH time to maintain the course, particularly during the rigors of World War II and the distraction of the burgeoning Vietnamese independence movement. By the time of Bao Dai's abdication in 1945, the course at Dalat was abandoned. Jim Sullivan of Mandarin Media, who helped coin the phrase Ho Chi Minh Golf Trail, notes that when local golfer Dao Huy Hach wanted to revive the course in the late 1950s, "he had to rely on aerial photos to pick out the putting surfaces" amidst the overgrown vegetation.

A FRIEND AND I WERE DRINKING IN LARRY'S BAR AT THE elegant Dalat Palace Hotel and I asked who the "Larry" was who gave the pub its name.

Turns out that a man named Larry Hillblom spent $40 million to restore the Dalat Palace Hotel and the Dalat Palace Golf Course – he could be considered the financial godfather of the current Vietnamese golf boom.

And there the story ends. Except I can't resist explaining who Larry Hillblom *was*.

In the annals of rogues, scoundrels, and guys whose life story would make a terrific Coen brothers movie, Larry Hillblom's true story is better than fiction.

Hillblom was a millionaire many times over – he founded and was the "H" in the courier and air freight company DHL. Besides golf he had another passion – he enjoyed deflowering young women, paying big money to madams in Vietnam, the Philippines, and Micronesia for certified virgins.

When Hillblom died, numerous women who said they bore children by Hillblom made a claim for his estate.

These women and children faced two obstacles – Hillblom did not acknowledge the illegitimate children in his will, and he disappeared in a plane crash leaving behind no DNA. Rather surreally, his home and office in Saipan, Micronesia, had been wiped clean of anything – a piece of hair, sweat on a sheet, a dirty Q-tip – that could have been used to prove paternity. The sinks had been scrubbed with muriatic acid, and toothbrushes, combs, hairbrushes, and clothes were found buried in the backyard, making them useless for DNA testing.

Considerable money was at stake. Eventually a judge ordered Hillblom's brother and mother to submit to genetic testing. After a lengthy court battle, four children from the Philippines, Vietnam, and Micronesia were awarded $90 million apiece.

I don't think this has anything to do with golf, but it's sure a swell story.

GOLF WAS PUT ON HOLD DURING THE VARIOUS VIETNAM wars. Nevertheless, American golfer Billy Casper, in Vietnam on a USO tour to bolster troop morale, played a round in Dalat with Dao Huy Hach (he was the guy who wanted to restore the course in the late 1950s) in 1966, several months before Casper beat Arnold Palmer to win that year's U.S. Open. "The course looked like it was just carved out of the dirt," Casper said.

GOLF HASN'T HAD SMOOTH SAILING IN THIS COMMUNIST country; Chairman Mao banned the game in China, calling it "green opium." Only in the last decade or so has Vietnam embraced a capitalistic surge that made golf not only permissible, but welcome.

Nguyen Ngoc Chu of the Vietnam Golf Association notes that golf had to receive an official Communist Party endorsement, that playing a game so closely associated with capitalism and colonialism was "OK." Because teachers in Vietnam only earn about $150 a month, and the prime minister's salary is just $300 a month, Chu notes, golf was seen as a rich man's pastime and had to be repositioned as being socially acceptable.

The breakthrough came in the early 1990s, according

to Chu, when then-Foreign Minister Nguyen Manh Cam attended a regional meeting and felt isolated when the other diplomats went off to play golf. Abdullah Ahmad Badawi, Malaysia's then-foreign minister (and subsequently Malaysia's prime minister), took Cam aside and encouraged him to learn to speak English and to play golf.

Cam returned to Hanoi and promoted golf among his colleagues. He had to overcome resistance, Chu notes, including a fear that golf courses would "take land from the people." Foreign Minister Cam helped to set up an informal golf academy for high-level government officials (paid for by multinational companies eager to get a foothold in the country). Cam took the advice to heart; he now speaks English, plays golf off an eighteen handicap, and is honorary president of the Vietnam Golf Association.

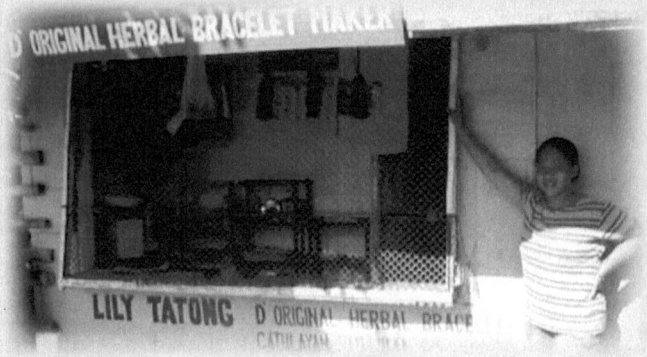

Win a heart, win an election.
All's possible with the right elixir.

LIGHTNING TEETH
AND SORCERERS

Ready-to-use potions help politicians turn on the charm.

SAN ANTONIO, SIQUIJOR ISLAND, THE PHILIPPINES

hat a wonderful world we live in, I thought. For just ten dollars I could buy a small bottle crammed with a magical potion made out of herbs and scrapings of "lightning teeth." According to Juan Ponce, the elderly traditional healer who created the concoction, the mystical brew will help the bearer entice new lovers. Enjoy business prosperity. Even win an election.

Moving slowly, ninety-seven-year-old Ponce showed me a cuspid-shaped chunk of basalt resembling a pre-historic ax head. "Very rare," Ponce's daughter Tata said. "These lightning teeth mysteriously appear at the base of the tree where lightning has struck."

Juan Ponce's house, in the rural village of San Antonio – Ground Zero for mystical happenings in the Philippines – certainly had the allure of a sorcerer's residence. Set up on a small hill away from the road, his wooden residence and overgrown garden emitted a vaguely uneasy aura in otherwise sunny and tranquil Siquijor Island.

Ponce is one of some fifty *mananambal*, or traditional healers, who live on Siquijor, a half-Singapore-sized island in the center of the Philippines.

Sorcery, magic, and things that go bump in the night are part of Siquijor's allure, along with lovely beaches, a forest reserve, excellent scuba diving, and a down-at-the-heels nineteenth-century Catholic convent, claimed to be the oldest in Asia.

So important is magic to the island's tourist development that the Siquijor tourism office proclaims the destination as "the mystical island." The governor of Siquijor Province, Orlando "Shane" Fua, Jr., offers guests small bottles of "love potions" made by either Juan Ponce or Lily Tatong, another *mananambal*.

Juan Ponce suggested that the potions are more than official giveaways. "The governor uses the potions while campaigning," Ponce said, suggesting that Governor Shane, as he is widely called, rubs a bit of magic elixir into his palm before shaking hands with the electorate. As I tour the island on the back of a motorized tricycle, I wonder whether it was the potion that helped Governor Shane win the last election by a handsome majority.

SOME ASIAN COUNTRIES PROMOTE "MEDICAL TOURISM." Siquijor promotes a variant that might be called "mystical healing tourism."

At first glance Siquijor, population eighty-seven thousand, doesn't appear to be a haven of magic arts. It's as laid back and as verdant as any out-of-the-way Philippine island. Some seventy thousand tourists a year visit: the Filipino tourists coming for a quick equivalent of a one-day Magical Mystery Tour, the foreign tourists visiting for the pleasant beaches and scuba diving.

I had first visited the island in 2001 with my son David and my friend Bill. I returned in late 2008, accompanied by Abner Bucol, a Siquijor native and research biologist who works in Silliman University in Dumaguette, a hour's ferry ride from Siquijor.

During our three-day visit, Abner and I visited half a dozen healers, and we quickly learned that there is no fixed route to health in Siquijor. Several healers, like Marcial Sumagang, a slight man with spiky gray hair and a frayed and faded "Hello Kitty" T-shirt, diagnose by checking the patient's pulse. One woman healer diagnoses by placing an egg on the afflicted body part. Other practitioners apply oil or wood chips. Several healers combine herbal treatments with printed *oraciones* (variations on Catholic prayers). And then there was the "bubble-blowing technique."

When we arrived unannounced at Genelou Magsalay Sumalpong's house, she was breastfeeding her five-month-old daughter. She lives in a comfortable, but not luxurious concrete house, and like most healers has enough disposable income to afford a nice TV and sound system. Abner explained that he had a cyst on his neck. Sumalpong, 24, listened, examined the cyst, and got out her simple equipment. She uses a technique called *bolo-bolo*, onomatopoeic for "blowing bubbles," which detects and removes evil spirits that are causing illness. The key mechanism, she explained after some prompting, is an ordinary looking oblong black pebble that she put into a water-filled jar. Her grandmother found the stone, "glittering like a crystal egg sitting on a nest," took it home, and put it on the family altar. That night Sumalpong's grandfather had a dream that he would become a *mananambal*, and a family vocation was born. Sumalpong placed the jar against Abner's neck and blew bubbles through a metal straw. The water stayed clear, and she declared that Abner's problem was natural; no devil was involved. Had the water turned murky with dirt, pebbles, and grass, she would have concluded that Abner had been infested by an evil spirit, necessitating an exorcism.

MOST RESIDENTS OF SIQUIJOR ARE QUICK TO DIFFER-entiate between "good" and "bad" mysticism.

Simply put, "good" mysticism, practiced by *mananambals*, is the stuff of herbal massage, traditional herbal medical healing, love potions, tourist souvenirs of "dragon's teeth" concoctions, heart-shaped carved wooden amulets, and colorful plastic bracelets to protect against, as one healer claims, "snake bites, voodoo spells, and vampires."

"Bad" mysticism, practiced by sorcerers, locally called *mamamarang*, is the "dark side," the world of devil-influenced spells. Way back in the isolated hills of Siquijor, people say, there are *mamamarang* who turn themselves into animals, who talk with the dead and concoct powerful poisons that kill on contact. At least that's the way Josette Armiola of the Siquijor tourist office, who acknowledges she "half believes" in magic, sees it. "Herbal medicines are good. Witchcraft isn't."

Armiola has a powerful ally in her "good/bad" differentiation – the Catholic Church.

Monsignor Larry Catubig welcomed me to his office next to the ruins of a two-century-old bell tower. He acknowledged that the Church has no problem with healers but does not welcome magicians. I suggested to him that Catholicism, like many religions, is based on miracles. "Yes," he agreed. "Miracles build. But magic destroys."

Pastor Dario Ocay, a Pentecostal pastor of the Blessed Hope Global Outreach, has a more draconian view of traditional healing and its associated magic. Sitting in an air-cooled room that doubles as the church's kindergarten, Ocay says, "It's all the work of Satan, and all healers are demon-possessed." Ocay's worldview is refreshingly black and white. He is an articulate and friendly man (he used to be an encyclopedia salesman) who admits that his father was a sorcerer. "All diseases are caused by demons," he says.

"What about something like cancer?" I ask.

"Everyone is a sinner," he answers.

BUT HOW BAD COULD THE "BAD" STUFF REALLY BE?

Evil enough to kill someone, if Telesforo Lumactod is to be believed.

We went to his easy-to-find house on the main road that runs through the commune of Ponong in the hills about half an hour from the slightly busier coastal road. There were no cars, just a few motorized tricycles and motorcycles. Village life went on at its own sleepy tempo – children played, chickens ran around, shopkeepers languidly chased flies from their produce.

Lumactod wore a green golf shirt and blue denim shorts. He is an unimposing Voldemort, with a wispy Van Gogh-style beard and missing a few front teeth. We disturbed him from his afternoon nap, a sensible pastime in the tropics. He was sprawled on a white plastic chair on the front porch of his concrete house, a half-empty bottle of rum close by.

"Yes, I can kill someone." Lumactod said.

Lumactod's modus operandi for mystical mayhem is not as straightforward as, say, Martha Stewart's recipe for apple crumble. His atelier is a secret cave, where he calls up wandering souls by incanting arcane spells, aided by a picture of the intended victim or a lock of the person's hair.

I thought for a moment about some truly evil people whom I would like to see injured. I decide to let Fate, whatever that might be, take responsibility for their future, and I do not engage Lumactod's services.

I asked whether Lumactod was worried about what will happen to him after he dies.

"I'm already in hell," the fifty-seven-year-old man says. But the rum confuses him and he rambles. "Heaven is only a story. And anyway, god doesn't give me food."

Lumactod also deals in more mundane love potions and concoctions to ensure business success. Could we buy one of his ready-to-use potions?

"Come back later," he says, explaining that his wife handles the retail side of the family business. She is a village counselor, and had gone to town on official duties.

CALL IT WHAT YOU WILL. HEALING. MAGIC. MYSTICISM. Hucksterism. The work of the devil or affordable health care? How did Siquijor become Grand Central Station of things that go bump in the night?

Perhaps the early Spanish explorers had a sense of the distinctive personality of Siquijor when they dubbed the island *Isla del Fuego* or "Island of Fire," because it gave off an eerie nighttime glow. No matter that this strange light came from the great swarms of fireflies that harbored in the numerous *molave* trees on the island – "Fire Island" has a pleasant metaphysical ring to it.

Vergie Bonocan Miquiabas, author of *The Mystical Siquijor*, says one reason for Siquijor's magical positioning is that people are poor and isolated so they turn to alternative medical healing. "And there are plenty of herbal plants in the forests that provide raw materials for the healers," she adds.

Of course isolation, poverty, and biodiversity occur throughout the Philippines, and other parts of the country have strong metaphysical reputations. But somehow Siquijor has jumped to the front of the queue when people think of magic, and a steady stream of visitors, including high-society matrons and high government officials, seek treatment and protection from Siquijor's practitioners of the gray arts.

Imelda Marcos, the imperious shoe-collecting wife of Philippines President Ferdinand Marcos, was among Siquijor's A-list pilgrims.

In a generally accepted modern legend, the first lady had a skin disease that resisted treatment by the best Western-trained dermatologists in Manila. She consulted a Siquijor healer who explained that Marcos's disfiguration was caused by a curse placed on her by angry mermen (brothers of mermaids) injured during the construction of the San Juanico Bridge linking Samar and Leyte islands. This edifice was hailed as a "love bridge," built in honor of the First Lady by her husband, a sort of modern-day Filipino Taj Mahal. At the urging of a Siquijor healer, the first lady made offerings to the aquatic spirits and her skin problem cleared up.

BUYING AMULETS IN JUAN PONCE'S HOME WAS THE rural Philippines equivalent of spiritual fast food – make your choice and take it home. I didn't like it. It was too easy, all cash and no soul. My experience with healers and magicians in Kenya, Madagascar, Indonesia, Thailand, China, and India usually called for at least a cursory discussion of my needs, at least the pretense of giving me something specially concocted for my situation. I found I missed the "personal blessing" aspect of acquiring something mystical. I wanted a human communion, not a retail transaction.

The commercialization of magic in Siquijor extends to the handful of talented illusionists who live on the island.

Arguably the most famous Siquijor conjuror is Vicente Tumala. His home, also on the main drag in San Antonio, is spacious, cool, and comfortable. When we arrived, a relative was installing a nightclub-sized stereo system, and a bossa nova version of "I Could Have Danced All Night" from *My Fair Lady* pounded out the massive speakers, shaking the tin roof.

Up until 2008, Tumala was the David Copperfield of Siquijor and was much in demand by tourist groups who enjoyed watching him eat burning coals, turning vines into pythons, and making dried, salted anchovies swim.

He's retired now. Tumala become a Charismatic Catholic, he says, and now believes that magic is the work of the devil. And he is still bitter by having been short-changed by a group of Japanese tourists, who promised him $120 for a dead-fish-swimming performance but only gave him five dollars. It's hard to tell which was the greater reason for his quitting show business – religion or cash flow.

REGARDLESS OF THE NOMENCLATURE – SPIRITUAL, SUPER-natural, magic, mystical, or just plain nuts – people around the world put an inordinate amount of faith in talismans, amulets, good-luck charms, and magic incantations.

Almost everyone has some superstition or quirk. Knocking on wood to retain good luck. Refusing to walk under a ladder. Changing course when a black cat crosses the path.

And who's to say it doesn't work?

BUT WHAT ABOUT THE VARIOUS AMULETS AND CHARMS from Siquijor? Do these things work?

I asked whether Juan Ponce used his own concoctions to keep him going. What's his secret?

"Just a glass of rice wine every day," he said.

I tried his rice wine – delicious but headache-inducing in the midday sun. But I had a more immediate physical problem than longevity – a chronically stiff lower back. I rubbed on some of Juan Ponce's *haplas* healing oil, which he says is made from some fifty herbs and ripens in a giant-sized Johnnie Walker bottle. My back felt better immediately, and the feeling of relief lasted all day.

Can we identify a cause and effect with Siquijor's love amulets? During a visit to the island, my son bought a love amulet, but he never used it; I will attribute his marriage to a wonderful woman years later to normal romantic chemistry. It's likely that a love amulet might give the wearer added self-confidence, which generally has an aphrodisiacal effect. I recall the sound-bite-worthy comments of Monsignor Larry Catubig, who had opined that the best love potion is the way you speak and your money.

Lily Tatong's daughter, Ferlie, claims empirical proof that her mother's love potions work. "Just look at my four children," she says proudly, as her cute kids scamper around the living room that doubles as a medicinal-bracelet manufacturing center. "Every time I wanted to have a baby, I would use this magic bracelet," she said. "With your husband?" I ask gingerly. "No. No need for husbands. When I need a man this bracelet is all I need." It was the first time I had heard of a woman requiring supernatural assistance to get knocked up.

BUT THE MOST ELOQUENT ANSWER I GOT ABOUT WHETHER amulets and magic potions work came from Siquijor's Governor Shane, the man Juan Ponce suggested used potions to get elected.

By happy coincidence, on my last day in Siquijor, Abner and I found ourselves having lunch at a simple open-air restaurant in the main town. The governor sat at an adjoining table with several friends and aides.

I waited until he finished his fish lunch and introduced myself. After good-naturedly blaming journalists for exaggerating the bad things and ignoring the good, Governor Shane happily talked about his plans for Siquijor and why people should visit his small province. Beaches. Nice people. No traffic. Fresh air. Marine nature reserves. We chatted for ten minutes, and I sensed he was getting ready to leave to take care of his gubernatorial duties. "Governor, is it true you rubbed Juan Ponce's love potion on your hands when you greeted potential voters?" I asked.

He didn't quite deny it but had a comeback that no doubt he had used previously. "I have something much stronger than any magic potion," he said. He waited a beat before continuing. "My personal charm! That's what won me the election."

ABOUT THE AUTHOR

Paul crossing a river in northern Laos.

PAUL SPENCER SOCHACZEWSKI has written *Share Your Journey*, *An Inordinate Fondness for Beetles*, *The Sultan and the Mermaid Queen*, *Redheads*, *Soul of the Tiger* (co-authored with Jeff McNeely), and other acclaimed books, along with some six hundred bylined articles in leading international publications. He has lived and worked in more than eighty countries, including long stints in Southeast Asia.

Visit Paul at:
www.sochaczewski.com

www.ingramcontent.com/pod-product-compliance
Lightning Source LLC
Chambersburg PA
CBHW020415130626
46549CB00006B/2578